MICHELANGELO
AND
RAPHAEL

WITH

BOTTICELLI - PERUGINO
SIGNORELLI - GHIRLANDAIO AND ROSSELLI

IN THE
VATICAN

THE SISTINE CHAPEL, THE PAULINE CHAPEL,
THE STANZAS AND THE LOGGIAS

EDIZIONI MUSEI VATICANI

INTRODUCTION

For visitors to the Vatican Museums, this publication has been a bestseller, and leafing through its pages it is easy to understand why. Written by Francesco Rossi and Antonio P. Graziano, the clarity of its text and thoroughness of its pictorial documentation gives the reader an insight to the artistic meaning and historical context of the two most important Renaissance artists, Michelangelo Buonarroti and Raphael Sanzio of Urbino. As in the 16th century, the works of Michelangelo and Raphael in the Vatican are still, at the end of the 20th century, admired by viewers for their timeless beauty and unmatched grandeur.

This publication is designed to bring the reader and art lover closer to the artists and their works represented in the book, some of which are not on display to the public. Its didactical approach with newly documented pictures and extensive captions make it a valuable learning tool as well as a beautifully illustrated book to be studied and enjoyed.

For this updated edition, new and unique photographs have been taken to accurately illustrate the magnificence of Michelangelo's newly restored frescoes of the Sistine Chapel including the Last Judgment. For this endeavor, the editor thanks the Museums' photographers, Alessandro Bracchetti and Pietro Zigrossi, whose skill and creativity in the production of the fold-outs depicting the Sistine Chapel after the restoration recreate the masterful execution of Michelangelo in its complexity. The section on the Pauline Chapel illustrates Michelangelo's final works for the Vatican which are closed to the public.

The chapter on the Stanze of Raphael brings light to details of the master's work and that of his pupils that may go unnoticed during a hurried visit to the Museums. Raphael's Loggias, which are closed to the public, show the reader a little known masterpiece in the decorative arts by the master and his assistants including photographs of what is known as "Raphael's Bible".

The editor also acknowledges the following people without whose indispensable collaboration and assistance this updated version would not have been possible: His Eminence Rosalio José Cardinal Castillo Lara, President of the Pontifical Commission for Vatican City State, whose vision of expanding the Museums' publications opened the way for the book's revision and reprinting; Carlo Pietrangeli, Director General of the Vatican Museums, for his patient guidance in the reviewing of the new edition and his assistance with the text of the recent restoration of the Sistine Chapel; Bruno del Priore, responsible for the original version of the volume that set the excellent standard of illustrative and editorial clarity as well as his collaboration on the new edition; Francesco Riccardi, Administrator of the Vatican Museums and of their Department of Publications and Reproductions, along with Georgina Bernett, executive assistant, for organizing the planning, research, and production of this edition; Fabrizio Mancinelli, Curator of the Vatican Museums Department of Medieval, Bizantine and Modern Art, for his assistance in the explanatory texts and captions; Antonio Maggiotto and Giuseppe Canesso of the Vatican Printing Press whose invaluable assistance in the project was fundamental in bringing the idea of the updated edition to its final conclusion.

THE EDITOR

Michelangelo
The Pietà

This famous Pietà is situated on the right as one enters the Basilica. It is the greatest work of Michelangelo's first period (1499). The Blessed Virgin, portrayed as a young girl, holds in her arms and contemplates the body of her Son, taken down from the Cross. The work conveys a feeling of profound calm, filled with sorrow and drama. Above: detail of the Blessed Virgin. On the sash across her breast can be seen Michelangelo's signature.

Interior of the Sistine Chapel

With the starred vault, by Pier Matteo d'Amelia, before Michelangelo put his hand to it. In the background can be seen the paintings and the two windows that were removed to make place for the Last Judgment.

THE SISTINE CHAPEL

The Sistine Chapel takes its name from Pope Sixtus IV Della Rovere. According to Vasari, he commissioned the Florentine Baccio Pontelli in 1475 to design a building that would house the palace chapel and also serve as a Vatican fortress (the crenellation of the battlements continues to testify to this second purpose). The actual construction was left to Giovannino de' Dolci—often mentioned in contemporary Vatican documents—who also supervised the pictorial decorations in the chapel until its formal inauguration on August 15, 1483. Designer and builder are both immortalized with portraits in Perugino's fresco, *Jesus Handing the Keys to St. Peter,* on the Sistine Chapel wall.

The interior of the chapel consists of a single long nave (13,41 × 40,23 meters) surmounted by a flattened barrel vault with spandrels and a lunette above each of the twelve arched windows. The floor is of multicolored marble. A high marble chancel screen separates the presbytery from the general body of the chapel. The chancel screen and the choir stalls, decorated in delicate ornamental relief, are the work of Mino da Fiesole and his assistants. The dimensions of the chapel, corresponding exactly to those of the Jerusalem Temple; the division between presbytery and body of the chapel; the original paintings—all these features testify to the Pope's desire to fashion a Renaissance version of the great Roman basilicas, with close ties however to the paleo-Christian and medieval traditions of the Catholic Church.

DECORATION OF THE WALLS

The original paintings, executed by a large group of Tuscan and Umbrian artists, make up a band of frescoes representing two great cycles from the Old and the New Testaments. The scenes were placed in symbolic correspondence in a high band that ran just below the height of the windows along all the walls. Below these, a stretch of simulated draperies framed a series of Della Rovere family crests. Only a fragment of this work still remains on the left lateral wall near the entrance. The remainder was painted over in the 19th century.

A series of portraits of the first thirty popes was set high between the windows. Of this work, done between 1480 and 1483, only the part on the lateral walls was preserved. In order to make way for Michelangelo's *Last Judgment* on the altar wall, the originals were destroyed; the paintings on the entrance wall were redone after the architrave of the Sala Regia door collapsed in the first half of the 16th century.

The Life of Moses

Originally, this biblical cycle consisted of eight scenes: six on the left lateral wall and two on the end walls. The first scene, on the left side of the altar wall, was done by Perugino and, as mentioned above, later destroyed. It represented the *Finding of Moses* and corresponded to the *Birth of Christ* on the right side. In the center, a panel represented the *Assumption of Our Lady* (to whom the chapel is consecrated) *Venerated by Sixtus IV.*

On the left wall, starting at the altar, the existing frescoes begin with the *Journey of Moses into Egypt,* a synthesis grouping several episodes into a single scene—a common enough medieval practice. We see Moses taking leave of his father-in-law; his return to Egypt; the circumcision of the second-born. The last episode is unimportant in itself but serves to balance and correspond to the *Baptism of Christ in the Jordan* in the cycle on the life of Christ. The Moses painting, not of exceptional quality, was done by Perugino to whom the overall design and most of the portraits are also attributed. The rest was executed by his most talented pupil, Pinturicchio, who was also the author of the lovely landscape, soft and shaded in the Umbrian manner.

The second painting shows several scenes from the *Life of Moses* (Moses slays the Egyptian; Moses puts the shepherds to flight; his vision of God in the burning bush on Mount Horeb) centered around the meeting of Moses with the Daughters of Jethro, one of whom becomes his wife. This painting ranks as one of Botticelli's masterpieces. He gave the central episode, executed with the graphic elegance and subtle musical rhythm that characterizes all his work, a mood of melancholy meditation on the frailty of beauty; and he re-echoed the mood in the romantic wooded landscape. Cosimo Rosselli, one of the less gifted of the Sistine Chapel artists, did the *Crossing of the Red Sea.* The contrast between the Hebrews—bathed in a soft sunlight—and the Egyptians—under the harsh clouds of an impending storm—simply lacks subtlety. The most interesting parts of the painting are the portraits done by Piero di Cosimo. Particularly notable is the portrait of Cardinal Bessarione, in priest's soutane, carrying a reliquary. The appearance of this figure gives the episode a "contemporary" symbolic meaning by suggesting the Crusades which this high prelate vigorously supported.

Again by Cosimo Rosselli, who was helped by Piero di Cosimo, is the fourth painting relating to the story of the *Ten Commandments*. The different episodes (Moses ascends Mount Sinai; the adoration of the golden calf; the punishment of the idolatrous Hebrews; the second vision on Mount Sinai; Moses descends with the Ten Commandments), overlap each other creating an effect of confusion and complexity.

The *Punishment of Korah, Dathan, and Abiram* —Hebrew priests who denied the religious and civil authority of Moses and Aaron over the Hebrew people—is an extremely fascinating work by Botticelli (whose self-portrait is the second figure from the right). The scene shows Korah, Dathan, and Abiram plus their families swallowed by the earth. The composition is cleverly done, contrasting the calm serenity of Moses and Aaron and the convulsive movements of the punished rebels. It takes place against an urban background in which such Roman monuments as the Arch of Constantine and the (now destroyed) Septizonium stand out prominently. An element of great documentary significance, rarely depicted in biblical iconography, it is meant to confirm the authority of the Popes conferred upon them by God. This intention is again emphasized in the corresponding painting on the opposite wall, *Jesus Handing over the Keys to St. Peter*, the first Pope.

The last painting on the left wall shows *Moses Reading His Last Testament to His People*. It too tells several stories: the testament of Moses in the presence of Joshua and a youth of the tribe of Levi; Moses sees the promised land from Mount Nebo; the death of Moses. Although Signorelli was very young at the time he did this painting, the same plastic quality and bold graphic design that were to characterize his later work are already in evidence. The figure of his young nude must have had considerable influence on Michelangelo when the latter worked on the chapel ceiling. This painting includes several portraits of unidentified contemporary personalities.

The cycle was concluded with Signorelli's *Contest over the Body of Moses* on the entrance wall. When this wall collapsed, the painting went with it. On the new wall, during the reign of Gregory XIII, Matteo da Lecce did a rather mediocre fresco, on the same subject, in the late-Mannerist style.

The Life of Christ

Originally, this cycle also included eight scenes. On the right side of the end wall, Perugino did a *Birth of Christ* which was destroyed to make room for the *Last Judgment*. On the right lateral wall, we begin with the *Baptism of Christ in the Jordan*. Perugino's signature was recently discovered on it; judging however by the mediocre quality of the painting, we must assume that it was more likely—and in great measure—done by his assistants.

The second painting, the *Purification of the Leper*, was done by Botticelli in minute biblical detail. The episode, of no great significance in itself—particularly when compared with the *Temptation of Christ* which was relegated to the back—takes on special meaning when one recalls that Sixtus IV once wrote a treatise ("De Sanguine Christi") on the cleansing value of the Blood of Sacrifice and sponsored various initiatives to care for the sick and invalid. He founded the still existing and functioning Santo Spirito Hospital—which appears in the background of this painting in the guise of the Temple of Jerusalem. In spite of Botticelli's unquestionably high talent for composition, this work is not among his best: all those symbolic allusions, extraneous to the episode itself, weigh it down unnecessarily.

The next two paintings are no better and are interesting above all for their numerous portraits and vast landscapes. The *Vocation of the Apostles*, by Ghirlandaio, depicts two scenes: the call of Peter and Andrew—both shown at work in their boat—and of James and John—intent on mending their nets. The presence of the large crowd in the background is a rather disturbing element: its only purpose seems to be to add those elegant figures and contemporary portraits to an otherwise static picture. The paintings of the *Sermon on the Mount and the Healing of the Leper* by Cosimo Rosselli have too many descriptive details. Only the highly imaginative and dramatically monumental landscapes of Piero di Cosimo stand out.

Recognized as one of the masterpieces of the Sistine Chapel is the magnificently beautiful fifth painting on this side: *Jesus Hands over the Keys to St. Peter*. Painted by Perugino, it was almost entirely executed by him (except for some of the secondary figures among whom Baccio Pontelli and Giovannino de' Dolci probably done by Signorelli). The scene centers around the group with Christ who hands the keys to Peter kneeling before Him. The keys are gold—symbol of the "power of judging" granted to the Popes—and silver —symbol of the "power of discerning". On either side, the Apostles and several onlookers form two converging lines with their slow, majestic procession. In the background, two symmetrical views of the Arch of Constantine frame the Temple of Jerusalem, a huge octagonal building surmounted by a dome that suggests the coming architecture of the 16th century beginning with Bramante. The wide open space all around the figures suggests an atmosphere of solemn peace in which Christ transfers His powers to Peter, His vicar on earth.

The final scene on this wall is the *Last Supper*. The setting for it is a many-sided hall with three windows. Through these, we see the three key episodes of the Passion: Christ's prayer in Gethsemane, the kiss of Judas, and the Crucifixion. For clarity of composition, keen perspective, and the dignified solemnity of the figures, this surely is Cosimo Rosselli's masterpiece. He rightly takes his place among the great artists of the Tuscan school.

The cycle was concluded on the entrance wall with the *Resurrection of Christ* by Ghirlandaio. After its destruction, another painting on the same subject by the mannerist Hendrijck van den Broeck (Arrigo Paludano) replaced it.

The Series of Pontiffs

Set between the windows in elegant Renaissance niches, the portraits of the Roman pontiffs provided a decorative complement once typical in old Roman churches, but abandoned for some time. In the Sistine Chapel, these works are not of high quality although some are attributed to unquestionably high talent (eight to Ghirlandaio; seven to Botticelli; two to Rosselli; and seven to Fra' Diamante). Twenty-seven are still in place, but four others (Christ and the first three Popes) were once on the altar wall and therefore were destroyed to make room for the *Last Judgment*.

Iconographic Interpretation

We mentioned above that the cycles of Moses and of Christ are closely balanced: Moses—who freed the Chosen People from slavery in Egypt—prefigures Christ—who freed all mankind from the slavery of sin. At times, the correspondence is obvious, particularly when single episodes are contrasted on opposite walls. But this is not always the case. We receive help from

the Latin inscriptions (recently discovered during the work of renovation) which run just above the paintings. The inscriptions were published in 1513 in a printed notice on the occasion of the conclave that followed the death of Julius II. With the help of the Latin inscriptions, the plan of Sixtus IV is very clear. He wanted to reaffirm, in strict theological precision, the close correspondence existing between the Old and the New Testament,—between the Kingdom of Law and the Kingdom of Grace. The series of Pontiffs logically belongs within this framework for they are the vicars of Christ just as Moses was His precursor. In other words, ideally there is an unbroken continuity in the life of mankind before, during, and after the Redemption; and this continuity is ensured even now by the presence of the Popes.

This then is the ideology, inspired by medieval Catholicism and theocratic doctrine, of the wall decorations. It was far from pure chance that guided Sixtus IV in his general plan and in his selection of specific narratives (for example, uniting events historically separated in time) from the old Roman basilicas. Insisting on his scheme imposed a heavy burden on artists formed under the new ideology of the Renaissance. Little wonder therefore that the Pope's favorites were not the ardent revolutionaries like Signorelli and Piero di Cosimo, but rather the modest and retiring Rosselli and Ghirlandaio or those who were willing to compromise, like Perugino. In conclusion, it must be admitted that this single-minded determination which subjected the will and personal style of several artists, this single point of view making the work of many artists one integrated whole, resulted in one of the greatest accomplishments of all the Italian "Quattrocento".

THE CEILING

In March, 1508, Pope Julius II called on Michelangelo to paint the Sistine Chapel ceiling which originally was blue with gold stars. Michelangelo accepted the commission even though he considered himself more sculptor than painter and preferred devoting his time to the monumental tomb of Julius II started in 1505. The Pope deserves praise for his choice; this artist, relatively inexperienced in painting, became the ideal interpreter for the grand undertaking.

Vasari reports the rumor, malicious but probably true, that Bramante had something to do with the Pope's choice. He thereby hoped to impede work on

(continuation, see p. 10)

Michelangelo
The Dome

The immense Dome, designed by Michelangelo at the age of 81 when he was the architect in charge of building the Vatican Basilica. When he died it was completed up to the drum. The work was finished by Giacomo della Porta, in 1588-1590, under Sixtus V. There is a wooden model in the Vatican.

Interior of the Dome

From the floor to the summit of the cross
the dome is 136.57 meters high
and is 42.56 meters wide on the inside.

the Julius II tomb and damage the reputation of Michelangelo who was his and Raphael's open rival. Buonarroti loudly declined the Pope's call at first and it was only at the latter's repeated insistence that he finally set to work in May, 1508. He carried on the task by himself, refusing even the help of laborers, while immersed in a thousand technical difficulties about which he writes in charming letters still extant. The work proceeded rapidly in spite of the difficulties. The first part of the ceiling was unveiled in August of 1511, and the solemn inauguration, with Julius II presiding, took place on November 2, 1512.

The original plan included twelve heroic-sized Apostles. Michelangelo even made preliminary sketches for them (now in the British Museum). However, as we read in his letter of 1524 to his friend Fattucci, he soon changed the plan. The complete execution, therefore—the structural design as well as the pictorial and ideological themes—was Michelangelo's alone.

The vast expanse of the ceiling shows up as a single coherent pattern made up of harmoniously flowing parts. No optical illusion is intended; instead, the painted architectural designs serve to frame and re-enforce the scenes. Vasari remarked that "there is no static view". He meant, of course, that there is not just one single spot from which the viewer should admire this or that scene; there are many viewing points arranged in chronological succession depending on the spectator's position and time of viewing. Above the main structural cornice is the lower area of the ceiling with spandrels and lunettes holding the "Ancestors of Christ" (except the corner spandrels which contain four "Miraculous Salvations of Israel"). In the upper part of this area, the run of corbels is decorated with "putti" in monochrome. The corbels define the intermediate area—that of the Prophets and Sibyls—and also support a robust painted cornice which is actually parallel (but appears higher) to the chapel walls. Finally, the cornice is connected by large bands to the pilasters on both sides of the thrones forming the frames for the nine scenes from Genesis arranged in sequence in the central area of the ceiling. Each of the colossal "Ignudi" (nude youths) is seated on one of the twenty blocks surmounting the pilasters.

Another feature binding the various elements is the pictorial plan with its own intrinsic logic yet innocent of any specific philosophical system. The neo-Platonism to which Buonarroti was privy in Medicean

Florence and the Franciscan theory of the "Tree of Life" should not be insisted upon here even though the artist's broad cultural and spiritual formation undoubtedly included them. The heart of the narrative is the biblical text from Genesis elaborated by Michelangelo as the myth of the Origin of Man. The validity of this theme today and for all time is suggested by the presence of the "Ignudi" who participate in the drama like the quiet, watchful chorus in a Greek tragedy. Beyond their literal meaning as part of the history of salvation, scenes are employed to reveal the state of man's soul after sin: sadness of uncertain expectation (ancestors of Christ); blind hope of a miracle (salvation of Israel); the profound serenity from knowledge of the future (the Prophets and Sibyls). Looking at it this way, we see the pattern on the ceiling as one gigantic spiritual history of mankind.

Histories from Genesis

The nine episodes are ideally divided into three groups relating to the origins of the Universe, of Man, of Evil. In the first group (*Division of Light from Darkness, Creation of the Sun and the Moon, Dividing the Waters from the Land and the Creation of the Animals*), God is the sole protagonist. He appears alone and solemn in the empty sky, and yet bursting with the energy which will erupt into a sudden, violent act of creation. In the second group, the figure of man appears fragile and naked in contrast to the massive might of the figure of the Father. Adam, painfully awakened from the torpor of unconsciousness, is snatched into life as if by a magnetic force; Eve responds to the sound of the divine command and assumes a prayerful attitude. In the *Fall and the Expulsion,* the inescapable connection between sin and punishment is thrust upon us by the fusion of the two episodes into one, divided and nevertheless joined, by the fearsome apparition of the serpent. The high dramatic moment of Sin passes from the barren landscape into an eternal dimension. Mankind is the protagonist in the third grouping as the composition becomes crowded, not unlike a choral drama. We admire the calm serenity of the *Sacrifice of Noah* as it contrasts with the dramatic agitation of the Deluge, that nameless cataclysm engulfing masses of humanity in terror and anguish. The cycle concludes with the *Drunkenness of Noah,* symbol of man saved from danger but ineluctably slave to sin.

The Ignudi

The colossal nudes are one of the most mysterious and ingenious creations of Michelangelo's spirituality. In their heroic nudity the artist saw the purity of man created in the image and likeness of God. They express intense vitality ranging from mute contemplation to crying despair, from melancholy resignation to mad terror. They sum up mankind reacting with all the sinews of its being to the mystery of man slave to sin. They mediate between God and man; they join the myth to the present moment in a meditation that knows no time.

The Prophets and Sibyls

Immediately below the large simulated cornice on the ceiling's middle area, on huge thrones framed by painted columns, sit the Prophets and Sibyls. They alternate on the lateral walls, whereas each of the end walls has only the figure of a Prophet. The ornamental scrolls identify them. Beginning from the back and moving to the right, we find: *Jonah*, in a state of ecstasy at the vision of God; the *Libyan Sibyl* gently turning toward the open book; *Daniel*, a beardless youth, intent upon transcribing what he finds in the giant book; the *Cumaean Sibyl*, face lined with age, absorbed in meditation; *Isaiah* caught in a moment of reverie as he turns his noble head; the *Delphic Sibyl* with limpid, wide-open eyes straining into the void; *Zechariah*, a dignified bearded man attentively studying a book; *Joel*, face matured through long spiritual effort; the *Erythraean Sibyl*, youthful, serene, about to open her book; the aged, turbanned *Ezekiel* staring at the youth beside him; the *Persian Sibyl* immersed in her reading, her worn features mocked by the harsh light; *Jeremiah*, bearded chin resting in his hand, deep in pensive contemplation of sorrow. Each of these magnificent figures is surrounded by one or more of the genii—the putti—who sometimes participate in the action or, more often bear witness to the Prophet's presence. By their various attitudes, they give testimony to the unceasing hope of redemption of mankind.

Both the Prophets and Sibyls see into the future: they represent that part of mankind which believes in the Messiah and which transmits its hope in His coming to future generations. It should be noted that while the Prophets in fact foretold the coming of the Messiah to the Chosen People, the Sibyls belong to the pagan world. The parallel therefore is superficial, based on their divining gifts. We see nevertheless that in the larger context of Michelangelo's spirituality, the expectation of redemption does not—and cannot—belong exclusively to one people. It must involve all of mankind.

The Ancestors of Christ and the Salvations of Israel

Not as well-known, but no less artistically coherent nor less pictorially important is the series of the "Ancestors of Christ" in the eight spandrels (invariably family groups of three figures) and in the lunettes between spandrels and the Prophets and Sibyls. These groups serve a double function. On the one hand they point to the coming of the Messiah as an historical continuity and reveal the divine plan for redemption as early as the moment of sin. On the other hand, their wild, terror-filled expressions and their evident pain reveal the sad state of the human condition after sin—ignorant of a salvation they cannot imagine. Thus, they represent an alternative to the Prophets who draw their strength from the conviction of an inevitable redemption.

The cycle concludes with the corner spandrels containing episodes in which the Hebrew people were saved by divine intervention: the *Punishment of Haman*, the *Brazen Serpent*, *Judith and Holofernes*, and *David and Goliath*. These frescoes have a specific pictorial purpose, for they serve as a link to the paintings below them (the Life of Moses). They prefigure the coming of the Messiah: they underscore the continuous presence of God in the life of His people and the constant renewal of His promise of redemption through the miraculous actions in dramatically desperate circumstances.

We mentioned earlier that Michelangelo worked alone, without help of any kind, even for the menial tasks. The stylistic variations that can be detected should be attributed therefore to his spiritual and artistic growth. When he began the monumental undertaking he had no great expertise in painting technique. True, he already painted such important works as the *Doni Tondo* and the cartoon for the *Battle of Cascina*, but a challenge in fresco was entirely new to him. He was—and wished to be considered—a sculptor; the mentality of a painter was not his. To him, a painted image meant transcription of a sculptured image on a flat surface; everything, in other words, reduced to the

Exterior View of the Sistine Chapel
Before Sixtus IV Della Rovere ordered Giovannino de' Dolci (or Baccio Pontelli) to carry out the works of transformation.

bare values of drawing and chiaroscuro. This explains why, in the early frescoes (the Noah scenes), the figures seem carved in the round by sheer force of design. Colors here play only a secondary role and the compositions are crowded as if the artist "feared a vacuum" but really because he had not yet mastered the feeling for open space. Having later mastered the technique (the creation of man, the Ignudi, the Prophets and Sibyls), he also mastered composition: the figures, isolated yet animated, radiate vital energy; the compositions are more studied, yet not mannered; the typically Michelangelo habit of contrasts is not limited to apparently painful contortions in the individual figures, but includes entire scenes vibrating in unison. Although the use of color is restrained—in keeping with the chiaroscuro technique its choice contributed enorm-

ously to the overall effect: he alternates disparate colors and contrasts the cold hard tones with opaque ones. It is in this part of the chapel that Michelangelo's pictorial language reaches maturity and becomes the only legitimate alternative to Raphael's eclectic classicism as well as the basic text for the dominant school of painters in 16th century Italy.

Not as obvious, but nonetheless of great historical importance in Michelangelo's evolution as an artist, is his work on the "Ancestors of Christ" in the lunettes. Here, the extensive use of contrasts (the "contrapposto") for expressionistic purposes, and of the harsh—invariably monochromatic—tones, create a feeling of cold torment.

This prepares the dramatic spiritual mood of early Roman Mannerism.

THE TAPESTRIES

The tapestries were an integral part of the decorations in the Sistine Chapel. Commissioned by Pope Leo X, Raphael drew the cartoon designs between 1515 and 1516 and sent them on to Brussels where they were woven with *Scenes of the Lives of St. Peter and St. Paul*. The whole series was completed by 1524 and hung that year immediately below the 15th century frescoes. After the Sack of Rome the tapestries were dispersed a number of times. They are now on exhibit in the Vatican Museums. Raphael's cartoons had another fate. After having been woven into tapestries several times in Brussels (results today in Berlin, Dresden, Madrid, Urbino, Loreto, and Mantua), they were finally purchased by Charles I of Great Britain on the advice of the painter Rubens. Today, they are on exhibit in the Victoria and Albert Museum in London.

Aside from their extraordinary artistic value, the tapestries had a specific pictorial significance in keeping with the themes of the chapel: the work and miracles of Peter, the first Pope, and of the first evangelizer, Paul, mark the historical moment of the transfer of the Gospel message from Jerusalem to Rome. They represent the justification for the spiritual primacy of the Pontifical See as the center of Christianity. The tapestries therefore were a purposeful link between the frescoes—that speak of the coming Redemption—and of the Last Judgment where the drama of a sinning and redeemed mankind is concluded.

THE LAST JUDGMENT

Twenty years after the completion of the ceiling, Michelangelo returned to work again in the Sistine Chapel. Paul III Farnese nurtured an idea—perhaps vividly recalling the Sack of Rome—of his predecessor Clement VII. The *Last Judgment* was planned for the present altar wall (in a conspicuous place, indeed, contrary to iconographic tradition) as a perennial warning about the frailty of life and the universe. After lengthy negotiations, Michelangelo set to work in May, 1536 (or perhaps even as early as the summer of 1535). The official inauguration took place at Christmas, 1541.

The focal point of the immense composition is Christ's gesture of Judgment. He appears high up the center of the wall, an open expanse beneath Him. Under the biblically awesome power of His gesture, a whirlpool seems to rise and engulf the entire celestial scene—saints and virgins, prophets, martyrs, apostles. We can identify St. John the Baptist (in camel skin), St. Peter (with keys), St. Andrew (with a cross), St. Lawrence (with a gridiron), St. Bartholomew (with his own limp flesh on which the artist painted an anguished self-portrait), St. Simon (with a saw), St. Blaise (with the wool-carder's comb), St. Catherine (with a wheel), St. Sebastian (with arrows). The vortex spares only the Virgin Mary, drawn into her own sorrow, and then extends upwards to encompass scenes in the lunettes —the "Exaltation of the Cross" and "The Instruments of the Passion". Once again Christ's gesture is the gravitational force of a second vortex that moves violently up and down creating a heaving sea in which angels and the damned, demons and the resurrected, appear to bob. Caught in the movement are the elect—who rise to heaven along the left side—and the damned—falling down along the right side while vainly fighting the avenging angels. In the center, the wide open expanse is reserved for the shrill of the last judgment trumpet. The open expanse serves then as a sounding board over which the excited agitation of the individual groups increases until it reaches the highest level of tolerance. Below out of the vortex, are two separate scenes. On the left is the resurrection of the dead, painfully and tortuously returning to life. Charon and his boat, on the right, epitomize in the oarsman's violent gesture and in the anonymous accumulation of cadavers, all the despair of hell.

The sources and meaning of Michelangelo's masterpiece were the subject of polemical conjectures almost as soon as the fresco was unveiled. Vasari saw in it the culmination of all Italian pictorial art; citing some of its sources, he mentions Dante and Signorelli. Pietro Aretino, on the other hand, malevolently criticized it, finding hints of heresy in it and denouncing the scandal of so many nudes in a sacred place. Unfortunately, his criticism found its mark: Daniele da Volterra, a favorite Michelangelo pupil, was deputed to "put breeches" on the nudes. What was the original like? We can reconstruct it by comparing copies, such as those (now in Naples) which Marcello Venusti sketched immediately before the veilings. The accusations and exaggerations, redolent of the Counter-Reformation spirit, explain some of the polemics the work aroused. But Michelangelo's was a tough, well-tried faith, a spirituality tested and lived in the context of the Renaissance but with profound roots in the Middle Ages. The pictorial inspiration is clearly from the Italian

⇨

Full View of the Sistine Chapel
With Michelangelo's Ceiling and Last Judgment and also the 15th century
frescoes on the lateral walls.

"Quattrocento" (Giotto, Camposanto di Pisa, Orcagna). In fact Michelangelo emphasized the ideal aspect by uniting time and space in a single vision and traditional divisions into sections. The drama before the viewer is unique and instantaneous and is acted out beyond time and space in the human sense.

Through this painting, Michelangelo relives—in spirit—the texts that modern experts point to as his possible sources: the Sacred Scriptures, the Divine Comedy, the Dies Irae hymn, and even the sermons of Savonarola. Just as for the ceiling, searching for the one single specific source inspiring the Last Judgment would be an abortive effort. We should rather speak of hints, of suggestions, which at times may even be quotations (for example, the figures of Charon, of Minos, of the devils shouldering the damned—all obviously inspired by Dante). In general, however, all the hints and suggestions were useful only in feeding the artist's meditation on the theme of death and judgment. Precisely because he did not adhere to a preconceived, rigid, pattern, but rather to a mental concept, Michelangelo could adopt the unusual, even heterodox, solutions that disconcerted his contemporaries: angels without wings; saints without haloes; horned and gruesome demons with grotesque grimaces. The images he conjures up are each a synthesis, almost ascetically pure, that has no significance of its own but only as part of that huge universal drama. Renaissance style is altered in order to express totally new subjects, an anguished reactionary spirituality, a warning as eloquent as Savonarola's on the vanity of things and on the implacable finality of the last judgment.

Conclusion

To summarize, the pictorial decoration of the Sistine Chapel covers four distinct periods extending across more than half a century. Nevertheless, there is an extraordinary continuity in concept and merits to be called "a plan designed by Providence". Overall, the various elements unite into one great cycle describing. the history of mankind—from creation to sin, to redemption, to the end of the world. This unity, however, should not blind us to the fact that each element is anchored in a specific moment of history and for an historically defined purpose; and that, therefore, it reflects a particular moment of Italian Renaissance culture.

The frescoes represent the Reign of Law and the Reign of Grace which Christ continued through His vicars. In terms of 16th century spirituality, this is the culmination of the history of mankind. In spite of the presence of so many artists in the Sistine Chapel—all in the Florentine humanistic tradition—the pictorial plans, the hagiographic content, and the didactic purpose are all derived from the paleo-Christian basilicas. This means that the culture of the papal court did not yet include salient features of the already widespread Italian Renaissance.

On the ceiling, Michelangelo's magnificent Creation, Sin, and Expectation logically precede the cycles on the walls; but the spirit in which these were created is totally different. Michelangelo saw creation and sin as dramas of all mankind, and the Redemption as an act of faith and hope achieved always and everywhere. Through the spectacles of his neo-Platonism, Michelangelo saw man unlike the one in catechisms or in the Sacred Scriptures; he saw a deeply profound spirituality. Along with the commemorative and hagiographic content of the paintings on the walls is the free profession of faith.

Raphael's series of tapestries, on the other hand, stressed the historical, not straying far from his own times. This was because the papal court wished to emphasize the source and validity of the Pope's powers as vicar of Christ. The continuity of the series on the wall—ending with the pontiffs—was done in an entirely different spiritual climate. The objective was to confirm papal authority at a time when Protestant Reformers made it their principal target of criticism against the Catholic Church. It is not by chance that this "historical" spirit prevailed in the Rome of Leo X, a Rome that claimed to be—and perhaps was—the moral and political capital of Renaissance civilization.

The last fresco painted in the Sistine Chapel, the *Last Judgment,* depicts not only the conclusion of all human vicissitudes—the moment when all who hoped for the coming of the Messiah or accepted His Gospel, or contributed to His triumph through His Church, find themselves together before Christ the Judge—but also, thanks to the tormented yet strong faith Michelangelo poured into it, an abiding warning to all mankind in the face of death. It is here that we find the ultimate expression of the Italian Renaissance; the bitter condemnation of the dream of universal beauty, where vanity is finally, and in fact, understood.

THE UPPER AREA:

1. Michelangelo: Lunette of the Ancestors of Christ – Nahshon on the right and his future wife on the left.

2. Michelangelo: Lunette of the Ancestors of Christ – with the aged David and Solomon on the left and Bathsheba on the right.

3. Michelangelo: Lunette of the Ancestors – Jehoshaphat on the left and young Joram embracing his mother on the right.

4. Michelangelo: Lunette of the Ancestors – Meshullemeth rocking Amon on the left and the repentant Manasseh on the right.

5. Michelangelo: Lunette of the Ancestors – Josiah and the little Jeconiah on the right, Shealtiel with his mother on the left.

6. Michelangelo: Lunette of the Ancestors – Azor and young Zadok on the left and a "philosopher" on the right.

7. Michelangelo: Lunette of the Ancestors – Amminadab on the left, a woman combing her hair on the right.

8. Michelangelo: Lunette of the Ancestors – Boaz on the right and his wife Ruth with Obed on the left.

9. Michelangelo: Lunette of the Ancestors – the child Abijah with a woman on the left, a sleeping figure on the right.

10. Michelangelo: Lunette of the Ancestors – Jotham and his son Ahaz on the left and a woman on the right.

11. Michelangelo: Lunette of the Ancestors – Zerubbabel and Abiud on the right, Eliakim and his mother on the left.

12. Michelangelo: Lunette of the Ancestors – Achim and Eliud on the left, the mother of Eliud nursing a son on the right.

ON THE INTERMEDIATE ZONE,
THE SERIES OF 24 POPES:

1. St. Anacletus, Greek (76-88) and St. Alexander I, Roman (105-115).

2. St. Telesphorus, Greek (125-136) and St. Pius I of Aquileia (140-155).

3. St. Soter of Fondi (166-175) and St. Victor I, African (189-199).

4. St. Calixtus I, Roman (217-222) and St. Pontian, Roman (230-235).

5. St. Fabian, Roman (236-250) and St. Lucius I, Roman (253-254).

6. St. Sixtus II, Greek (257-258) and St. Felix I, Roman (269-274).

7. St. Clement I, Roman (88-97) and St. Evaristus, Greek (97-105).

8. St. Sixtus I, Roman (115-125) and St. Hyginus, Greek (136-140).

9. St. Anicetus, Syrian (155-166) and St. Eleutherius of Epirus (175-189).

10. St. Zephyrinus, Roman (199-217) and St. Urban I, Roman (222-230).

11. St. Anterus, Greek (235-236) and St. Cornelius, Roman (251-253).

12. St. Stephen, Roman (254-257) and St. Dionysius, Roman (259-268).

THE LOWER AREA,
THE FIFTEENTH CENTURY FRESCOES:

1. P. Perugino: The Baptism of Christ in the Jordan. In the background: St. John the Baptist preaching and a sermon by Christ.

2. S. Botticelli: The Temptation of Christ illustrated in the background, in the foreground: the purification of the leper according to the rite prescribed by Moses.

3. D. Ghirlandaio: The Call of St. Peter and St. Andrew. In the background, Christ calls the two brothers and two other Apostles.

4. C. Rosselli: The Sermon on the Mount. On the right: Christ heals a leper.

5. P. Perugino: Jesus handing the Keys to St. Peter. In the background: the epi-sode of the tax money and also the attempt to stone Christ.

6. C. Rosselli: The Last Supper. Seen through the windows in the background: the prayer in the Garden of Gethsemane, the kiss of Judas, and the Crucifixion.

7. P. Perugino: Moses' Journey into Egypt. Moses takes leave of Jethro (background); Moses stopped by an angel (foreground). On the right, Zipporah circumcizes the son of Moses.

8. S. Botticelli: Moses Receives the Call. After his escape from the Pharaoh, Moses defends the daughters of Jethro. While tending the flock on Mount Horeb, he hears the divine command and leaves for Egypt with his whole family.

9. C. Rosselli: The Crossing of the Red Sea. The Hebrews are safe on the shore, while the waters engulf the Egyptian army.

10. C. Rosselli: Adoration of the Golden Calf. On Mount Sinai, God gives the tablets of the commandments to Moses (upper part). After his descent from the mountain, Moses presents the tablets to the people. Scorned, he breaks the tablets and punishes all who adored the golden calf (upper part, right).

11. S. Botticelli: The Punishment of Korah, Dathan, and Abiram who, with their followers, rebelled against Moses (on the right). Moses challenges them; when they fail, the rebels are swallowed up by the earth.

12. L. Signorelli: The Last Days of Moses. The law-giver proclaims the Law, after having seen the Promised Land from Mount Nebo, Moses comes down and entrusts the staff to Joshua. In the background, on the left, the death of Moses.

HIEREMIAS

AMINADAB

S·SIXTVS·ROMAN·VS·SE·ANX·
M·II·D·XX·I·MAR·CORONAT·
VR·AN·XP·IC·   II·M·II·D·XXII

S·EVARISTVS·GRECVS·PAT
RE·IVD·OEX·BETHLEEM·
SE·AN·XIII·M·X·DI·E·MARCO
RON·AT·VR·AN·FRAN·

S·CLEMENS·ROMANVS·EDIT
ANVIII·M·II·D·X·MAR·COR·IS
AT·VR·AN·XPI·C·

S·SCRIPTA·E·LATORIS   ✷·OBSERVATIO·ANTIQVE·REGENERATIONIS·A·MOISE·PER·CIRCONCISIONEM

NAASON

LIBICA

INSTITUTIO·NOVAE·REGENERATIONIS·A·CHRISTO·IN·BAPTISMO   TEMPTATIO

DELPHICA

AZOR
SADOCH

STI·LEGISLATORIS ✛ REPLICATIO·LEGIS·E 6 ANGELICAE·A·CHRISTO

IACOB

IOSEPH

ACHIM

ELIVD

IOEL

REPLICATIO · LEGIS · SCRIPTAE · AMOISE · ❧ CONTVRBA

12

ERITHRAEA

ZOROBABEL
ABIVD
ELIACHIM

OZIAS
IOATHAM
ACHAZ

TIO·MOISI·LEGIS·SCRIPTAE·LATORIS   PROMVLGATIO·LEGIS·SCRIPTE·PERM

10

CVMAEA

ESAIAS

EZECHIAS MANASSES AMON

IOS
ECHO
SALATH

PROMVLGATIO·EVANGELICÆ·LEGIS·PER·CHRISTVM   CONTVRBATIO·IESV·CHIS

4

IESSE
DAVID
SALOMON

DANIEL

ASA
IOSAPHAT
IORAM

PIVS·ITALVS·EXAQVILEIASE
AN·XI·M·IIII·D·II·MAR·CORO
NATVR·AN·X·P·R·DXXVIIII·DX·

OTHERIENVS·EX·FVNDIS
SE·A·N·VIII·M·III·D·XXI·MAR·
CORONA·VR·AN·X·P·I·CLXXXI
·M·XI·

VICTOR·AFER·SEX·AN·X
X·MARC·CORONA·VR·AN
·CC·X·XIV·D·II·IE

·SV·CHRISTI·LATORIS·EVANGELICAE·LEGIS·   2   ·CONGREGATIO·POPVLI·LEGEM·BVANGELICAM·ACCEPTV·   3

EZECHIEL

PERSICHA

ROBOAM
ABIAS

SALMON
BOOZ
OBET

S·ELEVTERIVS·XN·P·
QVISEANSAM·
RONATVR·PANS·DCCC·MIII·S·X

S·ANICETVS·SIRVS·FEANXIIII·
DHII·MAI·CORONAT·VRAN
XPICI·XVI·MAX·III

ICNVS·GREIXVS·ATHEN·
IC·SVIII·MO·DHI·MAR·CROONN
ATVRAN·DIC·LIIII·MDXX·S·

ISEM ✣ CONGREGATIO·POPVLI·9·MOISE·LEGEM·SCRIPTAM·ACCEPTVRI ✣ TEMPTATIO·MOISI·LE·8

P. Perugino
Moses' Journey into Egypt (detail)
Zipporah with her sons Gershom and Eliezer.

P. Perugino
Moses' Journey into Egypt

This fresco carries the title: "The observance of the old regeneration through the circumcision of Moses". We see an illustration of a passage from Exodus (Chap. 4, 18-20): After receiving the command from Yahweh, Moses takes leave of his father-in-law Jethro **(A)** and with his wife Zipporah, his sons Gershom and Eliezer, and entire household, takes off for Egypt. On the journey, the Angel "came to meet him... and tried to kill him" (Ex., 4, 24) **(B)**. Zipporah circumcizes Eliezer **(C)** while Moses and Gershom his first-born—observe the rite **(D)**. The convenant with Yahweh is strengthened and the mission of Moses is thus blessed. The identity of the other figures is uncertain, some, however, have recognized the features of Pinturicchio in the youth standing immediately behind Moses at the moment the latter is confronted by the angel.

S. Botticelli
Moses receives the Call from God

High on the fresco is the title: "The trial of Moses, promulgator of the written Law". We find episodes from the Book of Exodus (Chap. 2, 3, 4): Moses slays the Egyptian who mistreats the Hebrew **(A)**, the Hebrew helped by a woman **(B)** Moses escapes to Midian **(C)** where he puts to flight the shepherds who prevent the daughters of Jethro from watering their flock **(D)** and helps the girls **(E)**. While shepherding his father-in-law's flock on Mount Horeb, he hears the call of Yahweh. Removing his shoes, he approaches the burning bush **(F)** and receives the command to return to Egypt to free the Hebrews from bondage **(G)**. Armed with the staff of Yahweh, he leaves for Egypt with his wife Zipporah and his whole household **(H)**.

GEM·SCRIPTAM·AC

C. Rosselli
The Crossing of the Red Sea (detail)

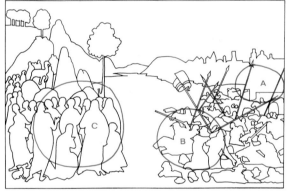

Above, the title resounds: "Moses gathers the people who are to receive the written Law". The composition, attributed to Cosimo Rosselli, is among those of the poorest quality in the cycle. Above on the right it shows the pharaoh on his throne while he is advised of the flight of the Hebrews **(A)** and in the foreground at the same time his horsemen are being submerged by the waters of the sea **(B).** On the left, on the shore, Moses, surrounded by the Israelites, commands the waves with his rod, while the people sing the canticle of liberation to Yahweh (Ex. 14, 27. 28; 15, 1) **(C).** Among the personages, to the right of Moses, with the red and white mantle and a reliquary in his hand, one can recognize Cardinal Bessarione who brought the relic of St. Andrew's head to Rome and in the 15th century was a great supporter of the Crusades and of the union of the Churches.

C. Rosselli
The Crossing of the Red Sea (detail)
Personages to the left of Moses.

C. Rosselli
The Handing over of the Tables of the Law (detail)
Personages to the right, in the foreground.

C. Rosselli
The Handing over of the Tables of the Law

The fresco has as its title: "The promulgation of the written Law by Moses" and condensed different episodes narrated in Exodus, ch. 31, 32, 34. Above, on Mount Sinai, God consigns the Decalogue to Moses **(A)**; Moses, having come down from the mountain is shocked because of the adoration of the golden calf, smashes the Tables of the Law **(B)** and severely punishes those who are guilty of idolatry **(C).** Having returned to the mountain, he comes down again with the new Tables which he shows to the people who are dazzled by the splendor of his countenance **(D).** In this work too Rosselli shows he is not equal to the task. His Florentine assistant, Piero di Cosimo, appears more gifted and the best parts of the composition are his; the portraits and the landscapes.

NEMO · SIBI · ASSVMM
AT · HONORE M · NISI
VOCATVS · ADEO
TANQVAM · ARON

Botticelli
The Punishment of Korah, Dathan and Abiram

With their followers, they rebelled against the authority of Moses **(A)**, refuse to acknowledge it and insist that Aaron is a usurper of the office of priest. They are put to the test. The title reads: "The rebellion against Moses, the Law-giver". The Prophet, standing before the altar, invokes the name of Yahweh against the rebels **(C)**, while their thurifers fall to the ground Aaron alone is spared by God **(D).** The rebels, cursed by God, are swallowed by the earth **(E)** (Numbers, 16, 1 sq), and their 250 followers are devoured by fire (ib., vv. 31-35). The building at the right **(F)** has been identified as the "Septizonium", still standing (at the foot of the south side of the Palatine) during the reign of Sixtus IV. On the Arch of Constantine, in the center **(G)**, we read the inscription: "No one may claim the honor (of high priesthood) unless called by God as Aaron was". The second figure at the extreme right is perhaps Botticelli.

SCRIPTAE · AMO

L. Signorelli
The Last Days of Moses

The title on the painting reads: "Moses explaining the written Law". Nearing his end, the Prophet sits on a throne **(A)**, with the book of the Law which he explains and recommends to the attentive people **(B).** At his feet, the Tablets of Mount Sinai and a bowl with manna **(C).** In the center is a young nude **(D)** very likely representing the tribe of Levi which was excluded from the division of the Promised Land: the tribe of Levi would depend exclusively upon the offerings received from religious worship. High on the fresco, Moses perceives the Promised Land from Mount Nebo **(E)** but he will never set foot there. He descends from the mountain **(F),** entrusts the leader's staff to Joshua **(G)** and dies **(H)** at Moab at the age of 120.

39

L. Signorelli
The Last Days of Moses (detail)
Moses entrusts the leader's staff to Joshua.

P. Perugino
The Baptism of Christ in the Jordan (detail)
Christ and John the Baptist.

41

OPVS·PETRI·PERVSINI·CASTRO·PLEBIS·

CHRISTO · IN · BAPTISMO

P. Perugino
The Baptism of Christ in the Jordan

High on the fresco we see the (recently discovered) original title and name of the author: "The Establishment of
the new regeneration through the Baptism of Christ".
"Done by Pietro Perugino from the City of Pieve". High
on the painting, God the Father **(A)**. In the foreground,
the Baptism of Christ **(B)** with a dove above His head
(Mt., 3, 13 sq). In the background: the sermon of the Precursor **(C)**, John the Baptist approaches the River Jordan
(D) and Christ preaching **(E)**. The identity of the other figures in the central area is uncertain.

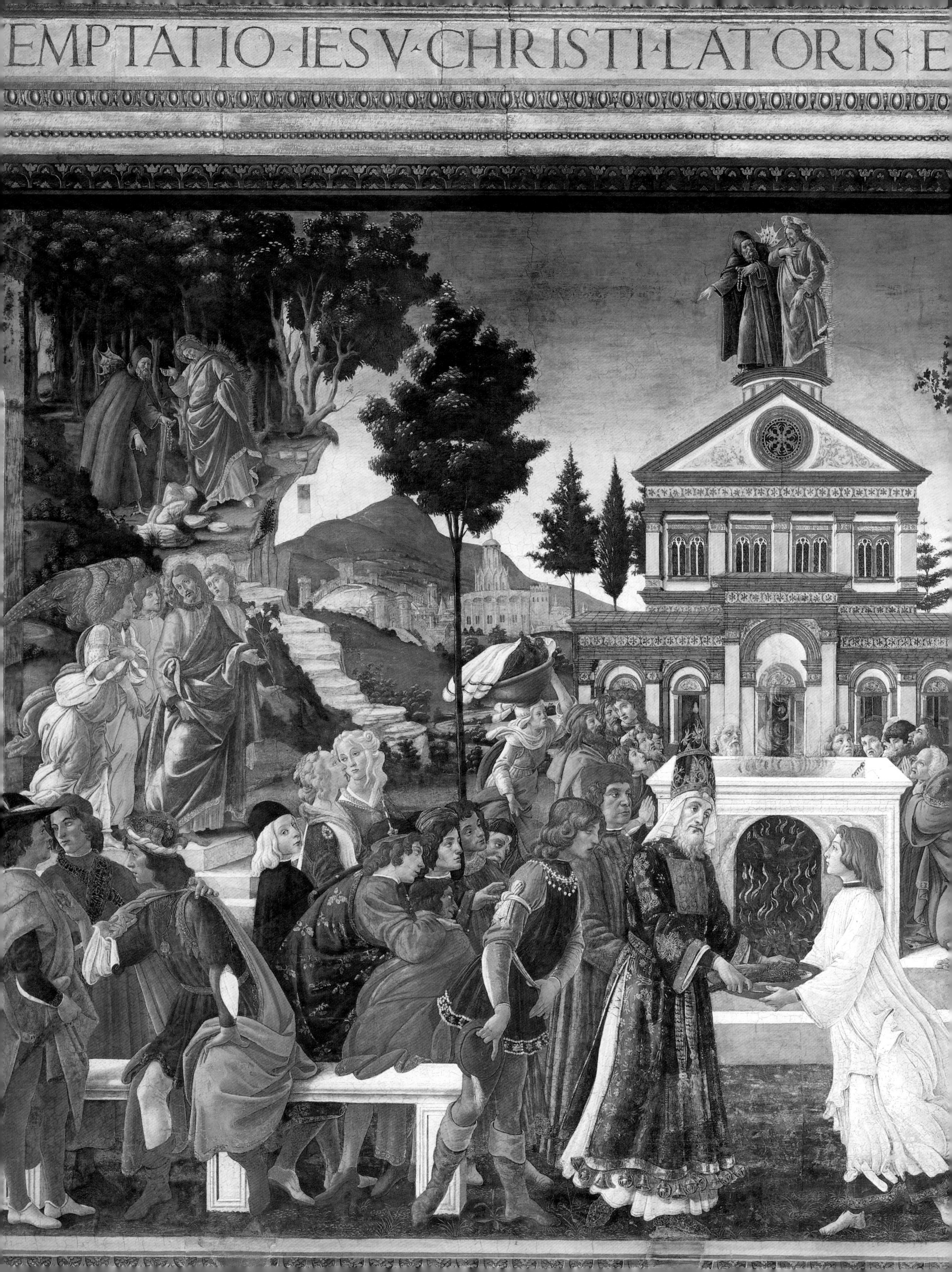
EMPTATIO·IESV·CHRISTI·LATORIS·E

ANGELICA E ·LEGIS

S. Botticelli
The Temptations of Christ

The title reads: "The temptation of Christ, the legislator of the Gospel". Satan, disguised as a Franciscan friar, tempts Jesus who is weak after His long fast in the desert **(A)**, he carries Christ to the pinnacle of the Temple and tempts Him again **(B)**; defeated for the third time on a high mountain, the demon throws away the robe and disappears. Angels draw near and serve food to Christ (Mt., 4) **(C)**. After Christ descends from the mountain, He observes the ritual purification of the leper **(D)** whom He had just healed (Mk., 1, 40). The complex rite takes place in the foreground **(E)** according to Leviticus, 14, 1 sq. The central building represents the Santo Spirito hospital in Rome, founded by Sixtus IV Della Rovere whose family crest is alluded to by the two oak trees. The two figures at the extreme left are probably Botticelli and Filippino Lippi.

D. Ghirlandaio
The Vocation of St. Peter and of St. Andrew

The title above reads: "The gathering of the people who will accept the Evangelical Law". On the still Sea of Galilee, flanked by a solemn landscape of trees and rocks, Jesus calls the first Apostles, Peter and his brother Andrew: "Follow me, and I will make you fishers of men" (Mt. 4, 18-22) **(A).** In the foreground, having left the boat, they follow the Messiah and on their knees give thanks to Him **(B),** while a large crowd of people forms up on either side of the solemn scene. In the background, to the right, Jesus calls two other brothers to the apostolate, James and John, while they are fishing in the sea with their father Zebedee **(C).** Large pliant masses and sculpture-like draperies show Masaccio's influence on Ghirlandaio and passed from him into the art of the young Michelangelo.

47

D. Ghirlandaio
The vocation of St. Peter and St. Andrew (detail)
Personages who are listening, on Christ's left.

48

P. Perugino
Jesus handing the Keys to St. Peter
Christ confers upon Peter the power of the keys.

49

P. Perugino
Jesus handing the Keys to St. Peter

The painting is titled: "The rebellion against Jesus Christ, the legislator". Jesus, in the foreground, confers upon Peter the power of the keys (Mt., 16, 19) **(A).** In the middle distance, on the vast multi-colored marble pavement, we see two episodes from the Gospels: the Pharisees seeking to compromise Christ about tax money (Mt., 22, 17 sq) **(B)** and the attempted stoning of Christ (John, 8, 59; X 31 sq) **(C)** In the background, the Temple of Jerusalem dominates the scene **(D).** It is in Renaissance style, flanked by two arches similar to those of the Arch of Constantine **(E)** which bears an inscription praising Sixtus IV for emulating Solomon in building the Sistine Chapel, and announcing him superior to Solomon, if not in wealth, at least in piety. Among the spectators at the scene, the following have been identified: Alfonso di Calabria (1), Perugino himself (2), Pinturicchio (3), the assistant Bartolomeo della Gatta (some say Baccio Pontelli) (4), and Giovannino de' Dolci (5), the architect of the Sistine Chapel.

51

·LEGIS·PERCHRIS

C. Rosselli
The Sermon on the Mount

The fresco bears the title: "The promulgation of the Evangelical Law by Christ". Of the four paintings by Rosselli in the Sistine Chapel, this is the poorest in quality. So many people crowded together gives the impression of disorder and damages the clear outline of the composition. On the mountain, in the distance, Christ is absorbed in prayer **(A);** at the foot of the mountain He comes down towards the multitude **(B)** who are spread out in the foreground; at the centre, on a grassy rise, He pronounces the Evangelical Beatitudes **(C).** On the extreme right of the painting, there is the healing of the leper **(D),** in accordance with the account in Matthew, ch. 5 and 8. In this fresco too, everything that is good is noted in the wild and grandiose background and is the work of the Florentine assistant, Piero di Cosimo.

53

REPLICATIO·LEGIS·EVANG

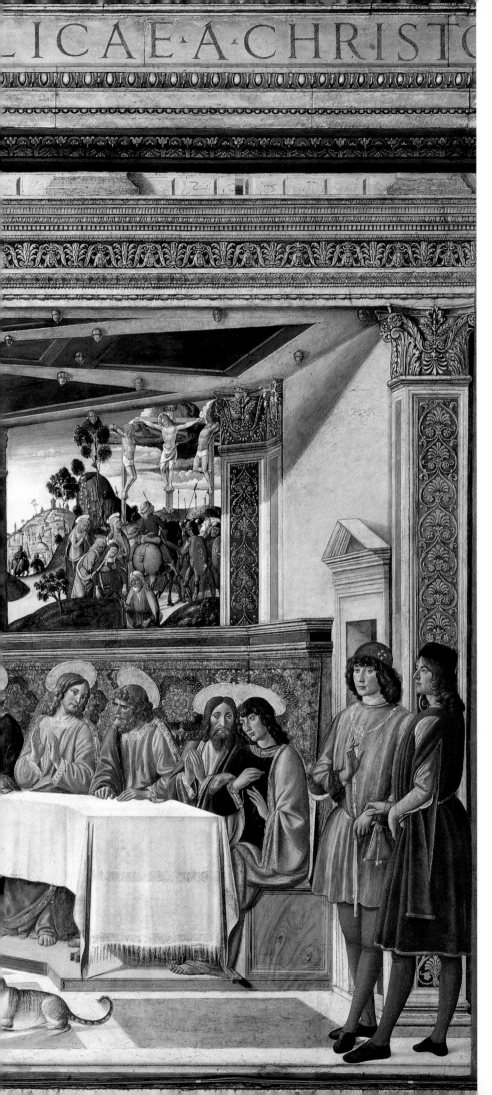

C. Rosselli
The Last Supper

The title above the fresco reads: "Repetition of the Gospel Law by Christ". In the foreground **(A)**, we see the Savior in the midst of His disciples blessing and breaking bread (Mt., 26, 26). Facing Him is Judas ready to leave for the betrayal. Unlike the other disciples Judas has an opaque halo and on his shoulder sits the demon tempter (Lk., 22, 3). Through the three windows from the left, the painter has depicted The Prayer in the Garden **(B)**, The Kiss of Judas **(C)** and The Crucifixion **(D).** The four figures on the sides have not been identified.

55

In the inside pages:
**General view of the Ceiling
of the Sistine Chapel**

THE SISTINE CHAPEL CEILING

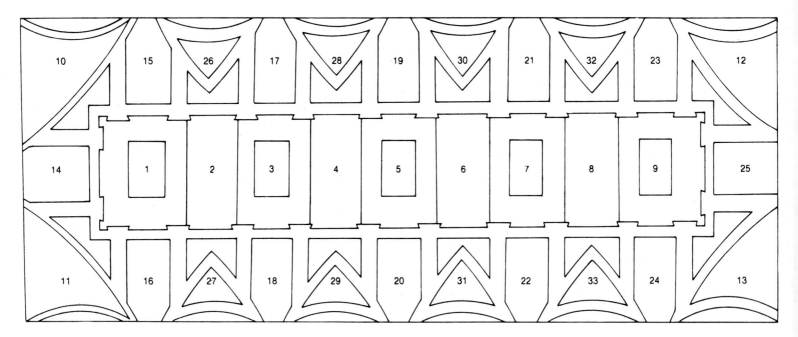

1. God Dividing Light from Darkness.
2. Creation of the Sun and the Moon.
3. God Separating the Waters from the Land.
4. The Creation of Man.
5. The Creation of Woman.
6. The Original Sin.
7. The Sacrifice of Noah.
8. The Deluge.
9. The Drunkenness of Noah.
10. The Punishment of Haman.
11. The Brazen Serpent.
12. David and Goliath.
13. Judith and Holofernes.
14. The Prophet Jonah.
15. The Prophet Jeremiah.
16. The Libyan Sibyl.
17. The Persian Sibyl.
18. The Prophet Daniel.
19. The Prophet Ezekiel.
20. The Cumaean Sibyl.
21. The Erythraean Sibyl.
22. The Prophet Isaiah.
23. The Prophet Joel.
24. The Delphic Sibyl.
25. The Prophet Zechariah
26. The child Solomon with his mother.
27. The Parents of Jesse.
28. The child Rehoboam with his mother. In the background, Solomon.
29. The child Asa with his father and sleeping mother.
30. The child Uzziah with his mother and father Joram, and one of his brothers.
31. The child Hezekiah with his mother, and father Ahaz.
32. The child Zerubbabel with his mother, and his father Shealtiel.
33. The child Josiah with his mother and his father Amon.

⇨
Michelangelo
**The Separation of Light
from Darkness** (Gen., 1, 4)

At either side, a twin pair of Nudes holding up two gilded bronze medallions. The upper medallion shows the sacrifice of Abraham (Gen., 22, 9); the one below depicts Elijah carried up to heaven in a fiery chariot (2 Kin., 2, 11).

Michelangelo
The Ignudi

The Ignudi are splendid youthful figures, each a masterpiece in itself. They sit on solid plinths alongside each of the five minor scenes. This particular muscular figure sits in relaxed contemplation above and to the left of the Prophet Jeremiah.

The first view of the complete Ceiling of the Sistine Chapel

After the cleaning of the frescoes, this unique view was skillfully assembled using 39 photographs to produce a faithful pictorial reconstruction of the entire vault.

Michelangelo
**The Creation
of the Sun
and Moon
and the Plants**
(Gen., 1, 11, 16)
The Creator
appears twice.

Michelangelo
**The Creation
of the Sun
and Moon
and the Plants.
The Creator** (detail)

Michelangelo
**Dividing
the Waters
from the Land**
(Gen., 1, 9)

Of the two gilded bronze medallions, the first has no pictorial representation; the second depicts the Death of Absalom (2 Samuel, 18, 9 sq).

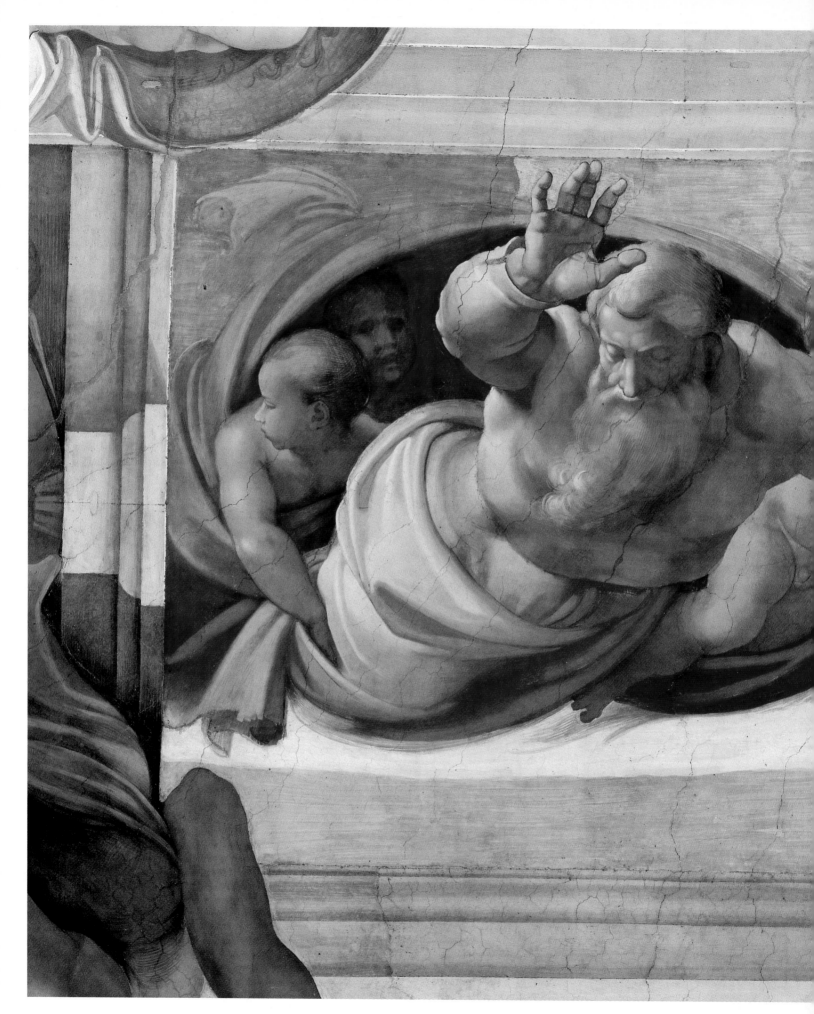

Michelangelo
**Dividing
the Waters
from the Land**

Sistine Chapel
Detail of the putti on the false relief of Daniel's throne.

Michelangelo
The Creation of Man (Gen., 2, 7)

Against the background of an empty sky, the Creator and angels. On the left, Adam stretched out on the barren ground. The only point of contact between them are the index fingers: the vivifying finger of God and the inert finger of Adam. From the outstretched arm of the Creator flows the spark of life. The artistic composition, completely original, possesses exceptional power.

⇨
Michelangelo
**The Creation
of Man** (detail)

Michelangelo
The Creation of Eve
(Gen. 2)

While Adam lies down deep in sleep, God raises the first woman to life. Eve, amazed, turns to Him in thanksgiving. The Creator, solemn in His full mantle, has a severe and grave countenance, the bare rock, the low and desolate sky, is almost like a nightmare.

⇨
Michelangelo
Original Sin
(Gen., 3, 1 sq)

In this larger painting, the artist joined the Temptation and the Expulsion from the Garden of Eden and divided the scene with the tree of life, a low fig tree, in the center. The demon tempter is coiled around the tree. Following the practice of medieval artists, the upper part of the demon has the shape of a woman. Adam picks the fruit himself; Eve, prompted by the serpent, accepts it. Justice appears in a flash at the right: a flaming angel pursues Adam with a sword. Eve crouches behind him in terror. Bitterness and disgrace now show through their once splendid bodies.

⇨
Michelangelo
**The Sacrifice
of Noah**
(detail)
The Ignudi

The Sacrifice of Noah

The patriarch leaves the ark after the deluge with his wife, his sons and their wives. He builds an altar and offers up animals in sacrifice of thanksgiving to God (Gen., 8, 20).

Michelangelo — **The Deluge**

This is the first biblical narrative Buonarroti painted on the ceiling. In the center, an overloaded barge is on the verge of sinking. In the background, the shipwrecked trying to grasp hold of the Ark of Noah (Gen., 7).

Michelangelo
The Deluge (detail)

⇐
Michelangelo
The Deluge (detail)

Michelangelo
The Drunkenness of Noah
The drunken Noah sleeps naked in the presence of his sons. Shem and Japheth cover his nakedness, but Ham, in the foreground, jeers him derisively (Gen., 9, 20 sq).

Michelangelo – **The Prophet Jeremiah**

The Prophet of the "Lamentations", worn out by suffering, wastes away because of the punishment that foreshadows the infidelity of Jerusalem.

Michelangelo – **The Persian Sibyl**

This countenance, like that of the Cumaean, introduces the "monstrous" in Michelangelo's paintings. Old and short-sighted, the Persian Sibyl deciphers what is written in the volume with great effort.

PERSICHA

EZECHIEL

Michelangelo – **The Prophet Isaiah**

The breath of the Spirit fills out the cloak of the sublime Isaiah. The artist has seized him in the act of dreaming in which he "sees" the Virgin Mother of the "God-with-us".

←

Michelangelo – **The Prophet Ezechiel**

On the Prophet's face one perceives the sudden anger against the prevarications of his people. He, suddenly, pays attention to the divine warning.

93

IOEL

 Michelangelo – **The Prophet Joel**

With an attentive eye he scrutinizes the scroll of the prophecies. In the wide forehead with the receding hairline of this Prophet, Buonarroti has perhaps handed down to us the features of Bramante.

Michelangelo
The Erythraean Sibyl

Visions of sweetness seem to pass over the pure and noble profile of this Sibyl. She predicts to the messenger of Rome a future of happy seasons.

Michelangelo
The Delphic Sibyl

This Sibyl, much admired for her physical beauty, is also portrayed in a moment of intense inspiration, with billowing mantle and far-seeing gaze.

⇨

Michelangelo – **The Prophet Zechariah**

Michelangelo begins the series of "seers" with Zechariah. Immense torso enveloped in wide folds, he reads and "sees" the Messiah-King entering Jerusalem on a tiny donkey.

ZACHERIAS

Michelangelo
The Cumaean Sibyl

This huge, muscular figure, daring in design and expression, shows the Sibyl—visage worn by time—pouring over her book. The Genii observe in silence.

⇨

Michelangelo – **The Prophet Daniel**

The Seer, with an elegant and vigorous twisting movement, is calculating the 70 weeks that are still to pass before the coming of the Holy of Holies.

DANIEL

LIBICA

IONAS

Michelangelo
The Libyan Sibyl

Here the Sibyl turns lithely towards a huge book ready to place it on her knees and inscribe in it the revelations of the oracle.

The Prophet Jonah

The figure of the Prophet stands above the Last Judgment. On the right, the whale that swallowed him and released him three days later. The episode allegorically prefigures the burial and Resurrection of Christ.

Michelangelo
Lunette with Azor (detail)

Michelangelo
Lunette with Eleazar (detail)

Michelangelo
Lunette with Asa, Iosaphat and Ioram

Michelangelo
Lunette with Zorobabel, Abiud and Eliachim

Michelangelo
Lunette with Achim and Eliud

Michelangelo
Lunette with Ezechias, Manasses and Amon

105

Michelangelo
Pendentive: The Brazen Serpent

Michelangelo
Pendentive: The Punishment of Haman

Michelangelo
Pendentive: David and Goliath

Michelangelo
Pendentive: Judith and Holofernes

Michelangelo
Severy: Hosea with his mother, father and brother (detail of the severy above Hosea)

Michelangelo
Severy: Solomon with his mother (detail of the severy above Solomon)

⇦
Michelangelo
Judith and Holofernes (detail) (Gen. 13, 9)

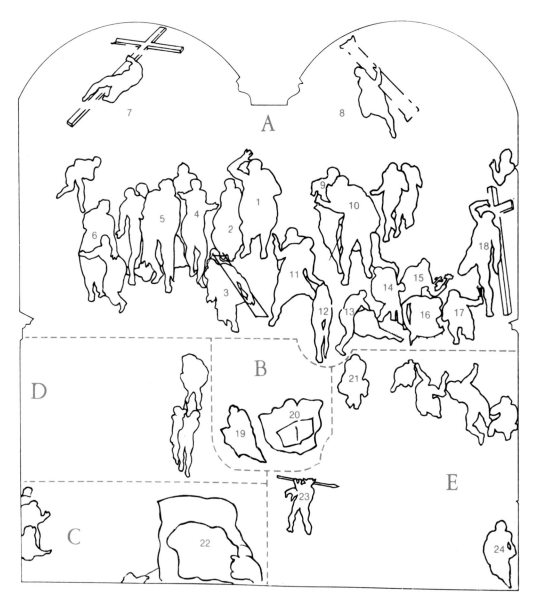

⇨
Michelangelo
The Last Judgment (detail)
Christ the Judge and the Virgin Mary.

All of the Last Judgment converges upon the figure of Christ, the Judge. He is the center of the drama, the eye of the whirlwind. Even the angels in the upper section carry to the judgment scene the symbols of the Passion (the Cross, the dice and the crown of thorns—the column of the flagellation, the ladder and sponge). The powerful sweep of the Divine Judge's gesture stirs a whirlwind hurling (to the right) the condemned downwards, and raising (to the left) the elect upwards. The result is a cosmic cataclysm: a confusion of bodies of heroic proportions and tortured passions; a riotous collection of living and dead made even more terrifying by the livid brilliance of the abysmal void.

Christ, His youthful body bursting with prodigious power, boldly leaps out of a ball of light and pronounces sentence. Alongside Him is the Virgin, eyes averted, her whole attitude one of compassion. On the left and right we see the moving crowd of Saints and the elect. The colossal figure of St. John the Baptist (not Adam, as some have said), animal skin over his back and sides, approaches Christ from the left. Immediately to his right and nearer Christ is St. Andrew with the cross. At the Virgin's feet is St. Lawrence with a gridiron, the instrument of his martyrdom. To the right of Christ we recognize St. Peter with keys and the bearded

(continuation, see p. 112)

A – CELESTIAL WORLD

1. Christ the Judge.
2. The Virgin Mary.
3. St. Lawrence (with gridiron).
4. St. Andrew (with cross).
5. St. John the Baptist (in camel skin).
6. Motherhood personified.
7. Angels carrying the Cross.
8. Angels carrying the Column.
9. St. Paul (red mantle).
10. St. Peter (with keys).
11. St. Bartholomew (with the knife).
12. St. Bartholomew's flesh resembling Michelangelo.
13. St. Simon (with saw).
14. The Good Thief (with cross).
15. St. Blaise (with the woolcarder's comb).

16. St. Catherine of Alexandria (with the torturer's wheel).
17. St. Sebastian (with arrows).
18. St. Simon of Cyrene (with cross).

B – ANGELIC TRUMPETERS WITH THE BOOKS

19. The Book of good deeds.
20. The Book of evil deeds.

C – RESURRECTION OF THE DEAD

D – BLESSED SOULS ASCENDING TO HEAVEN

E – THE DAMNED DRAGGED INTO HELL

21. One damned for losing hope.
22. The mouth of hell.
23. Charon.
24. Minos (with the features of Biagio da Cesena).

Michelangelo
The Last Judgment (detail)

The Elect, at last at their goal, fatigued but happy, abandon themselves to a display of jubilation (upper far right).
The one with the cross is perhaps the Cyrenean or, according to others, Dismas, the Good Thief. At the lower left St. Blaise holding the wool combs with which he was tortured.

Michelangelo **The Last Judgment** (detail)
Angels heralding the judgment with their trumpets
and carrying the books of good works and evil works.

Michelangelo
The Last Judgment
(detail)

To the left of the Virgin Mary, St. John the Baptist (Adam?) waiting in a group of the Blessed for the verdict of judgment.

Michelangelo
The Last Judgment (detail)

At the right of Christ, in a group of Blessed, St. Bartholomew displays the knife and flesh of his martyrdom. Michelangelo's self-portrait appears in the folds of the flesh.

St. Paul in a red mantle. Just below, St. Bartholomew shows the Judge the knife and his own martyred flesh (in whose limp folds Michelangelo painted his own doleful features). Behind St. Bartholomew is (perhaps) "Urbino", the artist's servant. Moving to the right, we see St. Simon with a saw; St. Blaise with the woolcarder's comb; St. Catherine of Alexandria holding the torturer's wheel; St. Sebastian with arrows; and that figure holding a cross while looking down toward the pit, is perhaps Simon of Cyrene. There are almost 400 figures milling around Christ in a tiered arc that gives an illusion of depth. Celebration and jubilation at salvation won are seen in the faces of the elect, in the embraces and kisses they joyfully exchange. Poised in flight just below the Divine Judge and over the infernal regions, trumpeting angels summon the souls to judgment. One angel carries the book of good deeds (on the left), hardly half the size of the book of evil deeds (on the right).

Bottom left, brown bodies struggle up from the earth and the Resurrected are helped by angels and saints to rise to salvation in the kingdom of heaven. In the meantime, a furious battle goes on (far right) between angels and the damned. The damned, desperately trying to hang on, are thrown down through the void towards the pit while brutishly grinning devils drag the miserly, the lustful, and "similar filth". The figures of the redeemed are light, airy, almost weightless: note especially the group lifted by the Rosary. The damned are ugly, thrashing about without care for the boat carrying them. The solitary damned, just to the right of the angel trumpeters, appears petrified with fright, totally oblivious to the precipice into which he is falling. Bottom center, we see the gaping mouth of hell and the porcine snouts of the demons crowding its entrance. The Dantesque Charon, "eyes like burning coals", flails his oar menacingly over the damned who plunge from the boat for confrontation with their own judge, Minos (on the extreme right). Slouched against a red background, ears of an ass and tail of a serpent, Minos supposedly bears the facial features of Biagio da Cesena, a papal assistant who rather imprudently dared to criticize Michelangelo's fresco for its nudes.

Michelangelo
The Last Judgment (detail)
Self-portrait of the anguished Michelangelo.

Michelangelo
The Last Judgment
(detail)

One of the damned
dragged to hell
by demons.

THE SISTINE CHAPEL RESTORATION

The restoration of the frescoes in the Sistine Chapel was begun in 1964 with the fifteenth century series depicting the Episodes of the *Lives of Christ and Moses;* interrupted in 1974, the restoration continued in 1979 on two frescoes of the same series painted by Mannerists of the sixteenth century on the wall of the entrance to the Chapel.

The plan was to continue the restoration on the sequence of *Popes* painted between the windows of the Chapel in the fifteenth century, but a sampling of the cleaning done almost casually on one of the lunettes depicting the *Ancestors of Christ* painted by Michelangelo revealed that under a layer of dust, residue from smoke and alterated glues had formed a blackish film under which were found the original colors, still intact, used by Michelangelo. It was also discovered that the glue which had been applied to the

⇦

Michelangelo

The Last Judgment (detail)

The demon Charon ferrying the souls to hell. Awaiting them at the extreme right is Minos with his serpentine tail and ears of an ass (caricature of Biagio da Cesena who criticized Michelangelo).

painted surface through the centuries, in an attempt to neutralize the effect of the above mentioned darkened film, was causing a degenerative "scaling" of the frescoes.

A cleaning and restoration effort was then launched in three time periods: between 1980 and 1984 the cleaning of the lunettes by Michelangelo and the series of Popes; between 1985 and 1988 the cleaning of the ceiling which actually took an extra year to complete due to its enormous frescoed surface; between 1989 and 1992 (extended to April of 1994) the cleaning of the *Last Judgment.*

A movable scaffold on wheels was built, inspired by the one designed by Michelangelo, for the cleaning of the ceiling; its width was limited so as to cover only a section of the ceiling at a time. Vertical scaffolding with multi-working levels was designed for the cleaning of the walls.

For the cleaning of the frescoes, widely used solvents were utilized. Thanks to the good condition of the fresco base, only basic treatment for the structural conservation was required.

The most exciting result from the cleaning of the frescoes was the uncovering of the original colors used by Michelangelo, almost always in excellent state of preservation, thanks to the artist's great skill in the application of "buon fresco" that he learned in Florence in Ghirlandaio's workshop.

The color palette which reappeared after the cleaning, and required critics to review what had been written since

Michelangelo
The Last Judgment
(during cleaning)

Detail of St. Peter with the keys of the Church in his hand.

⇦
Michelangelo
The Last Judgment
(after cleaning)

Detail of the right lunette
with the Exaltation of the Instruments
of Christ's Passion.

the eighteenth century on the artist's insensitivity to color, is normally seen in first generation Florentine Mannerist works and is the one used by Michelangelo in the *Doni Tondo.*

The restoration was carried out by the Restoration Laboratory of the Vatican Museums under the direction of Fabrizio Mancinelli; the work was done by master restorers of the Laboratory led by Gianluigi Colalucci; laboratory analyses were performed in the Scientific Research Laboratory of the Vatican Museums directed by Nazareno Gabrielli.

The restoration of the paintings of Michelangelo is but a first phase—the most important one—in the plan to conserve the frescoes of the Sistine Chapel. The second phase will include the series of the *Episodes of the Lives of Christ and Moses.* Very important results have already been brought to light with the first cleaning of the panel from the life of Moses: *Moses' Journey into Egypt* by Perugino.

Michelangelo
The Last Judgment
(during cleaning)

Detail with Minos, judge of the underworld.

THE PAULINE CHAPEL

There are few people lucky enough who, after having visited the masterpieces of the Sistine, can then go on to admire Michelangelo's frescoes in the Pauline Chapel, for it is not open to be the public being still reserved today to the Supreme Pontiff.

Communicating with the Sistine Chapel through the Sala Regia, the Chapel was built by Antonio da Sangallo the Younger in 1537, on the orders of Paul III Farnese, who was present at its solemn inauguration on the 25th January 1540, the feast of the Conversion of St. Paul, dedicating it to his Protector of the same name. Since then the new Chapel has been called the Pauline and the finishing touches were put to it in 1549, the year in which the Pope died and Michelangelo wore himself out in completing the final fresco.

The orders to paint the Pauline Chapel were given to Buonarroti in November 1541, when the Last Judgment had just been completed but was not yet unveiled. The old maestro who was exhausted took badly to the new task; especially as Julius II's nephews continued to harry him—contract in hand—to complete the famous tomb which had been too often interrupted. In a long letter to Mons. Vigerio, the bishop of Senigallia, an irritated Michelangelo wrote: "one paints with the head and not with the hands; anyone who does not have his own thoughts dishonors himself; because of this I can do nothing good while I have these concerns!". This time too Paul III intervened to silence Duke Guidobaldo Della Rovere (and he did so for good!). It was only then that Michelangelo, confessing that he could deny that Pope nothing, bowed his head and set to work.

As always, he worked with the help of Raphael alone who "ground the colors" for him. Having prepared some cartoons, he began with the *Conversion of Saul,* on the left wall, completing the work in three years. A fire which broke out in the Chapel in 1545 destroyed the stuccoes of the ceiling—a precious work of Perin del Vaga—but did not cause serious damage to the fresco. The following year the *Crucifixion of St. Peter* was started and was completed in 1550. The Farnese Pope did not see the finished work as he died in November 1549; but the previous month he had already visited the maestro, even climbing a ladder to view the paintings from close at hand. When he had finished, Michelangelo was already 75 years old!

⇐
A copy of the Last Judgment (Superintendence for the S.A.S.)
Executed in 1549 by Marcello Venusti, pupil of Michelangelo, for Cardinal Alessandro Farnese. The painting, measuring 1,90 × 1,45 meters, is currently preserved in the Museo di Capodimonte, Naples.

The two large frescoes (6.25 × 6.61 meters) were painted in the Chapel to serve as a severe warning and as a motive for the thoughtful admiration of the viewer, called upon to reflect on all that divine Grace had worked in Saul, unseated from his horse and made an Apostle on the road to Damascus, and in Peter who, in accordance with the prophecy of Christ, sealed his own faith and that of the whole Church with his martyrdom. Michelangelo felt the two themes in such a profound and personal manner, so close to his spiritual torments in those years, that they affected him even stylistically. The pictorial language in fact at first appears uncertain, worn out, of a minor tone, not worthy of the genius of the Sistine Chapel. To regard it instead with sensitivity, it appears rather as a new style, more mature and independent than the old tempestuous manner, with more wistful intimacy. It could be said that his painting, before finally silencing itself, still surged again and played the last card. The ideal norm of classical art which he exalts in the Ceiling of the Sistine Chapel and already tones down in the Judgment, binds him even less in the final works. He repeats, yes, the tragic effects of the boundless spaces of the transverse compositional general plans and of the powerful foreshortenings, but in a new way accentuates the anguish of the drama weakening the fluidity of the design and the extension of the opposing tensions. What also appears more obvious is the novel idea—already tried out in the Judgment—of abolishing the limits of the wall in order to suggest to the viewer a wider external space. Because of this, in the Pauline Chapel, the personages on the sides, the soldiers who are advancing upwards and are seen from behind and the weeping women, appear to be cut.

The *Conversion of Saul* faithfully recounts all that is said in the Acts of the Apostles 9, 22, 26.

The scene on top is completely decentralized to the left with the subsequent creation of a large empty space to the right. Surrounded by the wingless angels, Christ, with His arm outstretched, casts a ray of light on the persecutor and while He apostrophizes him —"Saul, Saul, why do you persecute me?"—with His left arm indicates the nearby Damascus. Saul, overcome, falls blinded to the ground, covers his face bathed in light and exclaims: "Lord, what do you want me to do?". All around, the soldiers seized with panic hear the voice but do not see anyone and flee into the empty background. Some of them fall to the ground. Some try to hold back the plumed horse.

Saul and his pitiful companion, at the center of the scene, seem to be dealt with perfectly by the painter with respect to the other characters, some of whom are drawn in a perfunctory way. While on the painting

(continuation, see p. 129)

MIHI VIVERE
CHRISTVS EST
ET MORI LVCRVM

the ray of light works an unusual burst of color, the very agitation of the surrounding characters accentuates the drama in the foreground, in which Michelangelo's torment seems to have lost weight, to the point of bestowing on the renewed Paul his already elderly features. The *Crucifixion of St. Peter* differs profoundly from the *Conversion of Saul,* because it evokes a calmer climate and a more human vision of the event. While in the first fresco the movement of the characters tends to separate the groups, here instead the figures are gathered around the enormous cross which cuts the wall diagonally. The Apostle Peter, a giant of the faith, is hanging with his head downwards and Michelangelo, as he did for the Saul group, has drawn him with a masterly hand. In the difficult foreshortening, the martyr with a fulminating look and an heroic gesture, turns to the viewer almost as if to warn him severely that such a great sacrifice should not be rendered vain. An empty sky overhangs the sad procession of figures who silently descend to the bottom, hardly giving a glance to the cross which, shortly, when the light-colored pit has been dug, will go into the deep hole.

On this wall too the color is different and more vivacious than in the other; and yet it appears that only four were used in it: red, yellow, green and blue. But the maestro used them in such a way as to model the bodies and clothes of the characters with chiaroscuro alone. With thick, subtle and sure brush-strokes he obtained effects such as those of a mallet on marble.

Michelangelo aroused no enthusiasm for these final frescoes in his own day. Too often—more than in the Judgment!—he distanced himself from the classical ideal, which was considered to have remained unchanged since the time of the Renaissance! After the Pauline Chapel he, having laid down his brushes, sculptured his last disconsolate *Pietàs.* "For the love of God and without any recompense" he strove to complete the new Basilica of St. Peter and to raise the stupendous Dome. Until, on the 18th February 1564, with his death he passed "from the horrible tempest to sweet calm".

Michelangelo
The Pauline Chapel. Overall view

In 1537 Paul III had it built by Antonio Sangallo the Younger as the Pope's private chapel and dedicated it to the Apostle of the Gentiles on the 25th January 1540, the feast of the Conversion of St. Paul. It has a robust line on a rectangular plan, more restricted approaching the altar. The stuccoes on the Ceiling, dating back to the time of Gregory XIII, cannot be compared with those splendid ones by Perin del Vaga, Raphael s assistant in the Loggias, destroyed by the fire which broke out in the Chapel in 1545, while Michelangelo was frescoing the walls. Also of a later date are the paintings by L. Sabatini and F. Zuccari, truly a jarring note in this Chapel which houses the last precious frescoes of Buonarroti, the *Conversion of Saul* and the *Crucifixion of St. Peter,* visible on the sides, in the foreground.

Michelangelo
The Conversion of Saul

The fresco, seen as a whole, obviously demonstrates Michelangelo's new style which, more than in the Sistine Chapel, contrasts with the ideals of classicism. The composition is completely moved to the left with respect to the axis of the wall and attention is drawn downwards to the drama — Saul fallen to the ground and given assistance — towards which both the general plan of the composition and also the movement relate, as well as the soothing plasticity of the groups and the color. The two soldiers who enter "into the field" from below, are a new way of making the composition free and easy and involving the viewer in the event.

⇨

Michelangelo
The Conversion of Saul (detail)

Saul, blinded by the light, is assisted by a companion, the only one who bends down to help him. It is the central group of the composition and as such particular care is given to it by the maestro. The face, old and with a flowing beard, is certainly not due to biblical "license", unforgivable for a reader of the Bible like Michelangelo, but rather to the way the seventy year-old maestro recognized himself in the torment of the protagonist, to the point of giving him his own features. And so we have his final "instantaneous" physical and spiritual portrait.

Michelangelo
The Crucifixion of St. Peter

When Paul III ordered the frescoes for the Pauline Chapel, it appears that
he wanted a *Handing over of the Keys* opposite the *Conversion of Saul*,
the two moments of the calling of Peter and Paul to the apostolate. How
the subject came to be changed with the present one we do not know.
Perhaps Michelangelo himself was not extraneous to the variation, wan-
ting a theme that was more consonant with his art. The *Crucifixion of
St. Peter* is profoundly different from the preceding fresco. The general ar-
rangement is more balanced, the sky weighs down on a mass of completely anonymous figures, except for a few characters who stand out: the
soldiers who are going up to the left, the young man who is protesting,
the giant on the right, the small group of women. The rest is silent expectation that the sacrifice of Peter, the hero of the faith who offered himself
to confirm the faith of his brethren, will be consummated.

⇨
Michelangelo
The Crucifixion of St. Peter (detail)

At the center the crucifiers are ready to work from behind to rotate the
enormous transversal cross and push it into the hole. Their gesture im-
prints a turning movement on the whole composition. But everything is
dominated by the naked body of the martyr, perfectly modelled and of
exceptional power. It was Christ Himself who predicted his death on the
cross to the fiery martyr. That at the moment of his excecution Peter felt
himself unworthy to die in the same position as the Master and chose to
be crucified upside down, we have only from a long and ancient tradition
and from Jacopo da Voragine's *Legenda Aurea*.

Michelangelo
The Crucifixion of St. Peter (detail)

This band of sorrowing Christian women, much admired in the fresco, has been cut off below from the end of the wall. It is a new contrivance by the painter to suggest a wider external space to the viewer and was repeated in other figures of the last two frescoes. The mournful group draws the eye towards the opposite hill where the centurion on horseback issues orders. He makes his comments on the outrage in a submissive tone and makes haste to leave the scene.

THE RAPHAEL STANZAS

Raphael Sanzio was only twenty-five when he left Florence for Rome in 1508 to paint the frescoes in the new apartments the Holy Father chose to occupy. The commission was given by Julius II Della Rovere who no longer cared to stay in the rooms once occupied by his predecessor, Alexander VI Borgia. He took instead a four room apartment on the top floor. Three of the four rooms were of modest dimensions and had once served as part of the residence of Pope Nicholas V. The fourth was considerably larger and dated back to the 13th century Pope, Nicholas III. With the completion of the work, these rooms were forever afterwards called "The Raphael Stanzas". They comprise the *Stanza of the Borgo Fire*, the *Stanza of the Signatura*, the *Stanza of Heliodorus*, and the *Stanza of Constantine*. At the turn of the 15th century, several artists collaborated in decorating the rooms. They were Piero della Francesca, Bramantino, Fra' Bartolomeo della Gatta, and Luca Signorelli. Julius II also called upon Sodoma, Lorenzo Lotto, and Perugino to complete the work. But when Raphael arrived in Rome at the end of 1508, he himself ordered the works destroyed. This signalled the beginning of the richest and greatest series of Renaissance paintings from the stand-point both of doctrinal content and stylistic development.

I. The Stanza of the Signatura
(1508-1511)

No doubt it was a scholar of the papal court—someone of the stature of Calcagnini, Ariosto, or Inghirami—who, with papal approval, planned the decorative theme

(continuation, see p. 139)

THE DISPUTE ON THE BLESSED SACRAMENT

A — TOP SECTION

    1. The Eternal Father.
    2. The Word Incarnate.
    3. Angels.
    4. The Virgin Mary.
    5. St. John the Baptist.

B — MIDDLE SECTION

    6. St. Peter.
    7. Adam.
    8. St. John the Evangelist.
    9. David.
   10. St. Lawrence.
   11. Jeremiah (?).
   12. Angels with the Gospels.
   13. The Holy Spirit.
   14. Judas Maccabeus (?).
   15. St. Stephen.
   16. Moses.

   17. St. James the Lesser.
   18. Abraham.
   19. St. Paul.

C — LOWER SECTION

   20. Blessed Fra' Angelico.
   21. Bramante.
   22. Francesco Maria Della Rovere.
   23. St. Gregory the Great (features of Julius II).
   24. St. Jerome.
   25. St. Ambrose.
   26. St. Augustine.
   27. St. Thomas Aquinas.
   28. Innocent III.
   29. St. Bonaventure.
   30. Sixtus IV.
   31. Dante.
   32. Girolamo Savonarola

Raphael
**The Stanza
of the Signatura.
View of the Stanza
with the Dispute on
the Blessed Sacra-
ment**

Raphael
**The Stanza of the Signatura.
The Dispute on the Blessed
Sacrament** (detail)

Portrait of Blessed Fra' Angelico.

⇨
Raphael
**The Stanza of the Signatura.
The Dispute on the Blessed
Sacrament** (detail)

The Holy Trinity, the Virgin Mary,
St. John the Baptist, and four angels
with the Gospels.

for the first room Raphael was to fresco. The decision was taken: the great neo-Platonic concepts of Truth, Good, and Beauty would be glorified in painting. This distinctively humanistic theme was probably selected in view of the eventual use destined for the room: it was to serve as the Pope's library, or so Paolo Giovio, writing at the time, informs us.

The room became known as the *Stanza of the Signatura* because as soon at the work was completed, the most important papal documents were signed and sealed here. The frescoed walls represent the major masterpieces personally painted by the young master from Urbino—The *Dispute on the Blessed Sacrament* and the *School of Athens*—exalting revealed Truth and natural Truth. The concept of Beauty, inspired by poetry, is depicted in the *Mount Parnassus* fresco. Good is pictorially represented in the *Theological and Cardinal Virtues* and in *Law,* both ecclesiastical (*St. Raymond of Peñafort Presenting the Decretals to Gregory IX*) and civil (*The Emperor Justinian Handing the Pandects to Trebonianus*). The decoration of the ceiling re-echoes the same concepts by personifying them.

Raphael rejected abstractions, symbols, and allegories in pictorially interpreting the universal concepts of Truth, Beauty, and Good; instead, his creative and innovative genius, seized upon "illustrious personalities" who, in the flesh give movement, light, color, and life to the philosophical content of these abstract concepts.

"Triumph of the Church and of the Faith" would be a more suitable title for the scene of the *Dis-*

Raphael
**The Stanza of the Signatura.
The Dispute on the Blessed Sacrament**

pute on the Blessed Sacrament. In this fresco, in fact, Raphael shows us God, the Supreme Truth, contemplated in beatific vision in heaven and adored in faith on earth under the appearance of the consecrated Host. The focal point, the core of the pictorial composition where all the lines of vision converge, is the Eucharistic Bread. The Eucharist—Heaven's own loving gift to the world and at the same time an invitation to join the Holy Trinity—is on an axis that joins the Host to the Trinity. Around this central axis, deployed in a double layer of semicircles, the whole Church militant and triumphant gathers in contemplation.

At the top of the lunette, the Eternal Father appears in the act of blessing between two choirs of angels. Immediately below, surrounded by a great aureola, is His Incarnate Son, the adoring Madonna in an attitude of prayer, and St. John the Baptist. Below these figures is the Holy Spirit, the Inspirer of the four Gospels pictured as open books. Seated on clouds on either side of the central group are the Blessed of the Old and the New Testament—the Church triumphant. We see, from the left, St. Peter, Adam, St. John the Evangelist, David, St. Lawrence, and a prophet; on the right, Judas Maccabee (?), St. Stephen, Moses, St. James the Lesser, Abraham, and St. Paul. Each is recognized by some characteristic detail.

In the lower band of the fresco we see the Fathers of the Church and several theologians—the Church militant—discussing the

(continuation, see p. 146)

Raphael
**The Stanza of the Signatura.
The Dispute on the Blessed
Sacrament**

Group of theologians among whom are St. Gregory the Great and St. Jerome.

140

Raphael
**The Stanza of the Signatura.
The Dispute on the Blessed
Sacrament** (detail)

In the group of theologians are St. Bonaventure, St. Thomas and Pope Sixtus IV.

⇨
Raphael
**The Stanza of the Signatura.
The Dispute on the Blessed
Sacrament** (detail)

A group of people among whom are the Blessed Fra' Angelico, Bramante, and Francesco Maria Della Rovere.

THE SCHOOL OF ATHENS

1. Plato (Leonardo da Vinci).
2. Aristotle.
3. Socrates.
4. Xenofon.
5. Aeschines (Alcibiades?).
6. Alcibiades (Alexander?).
7. Zeno.
8. Epicurus.
9. Federico Gonzaga.
10. Averroes.
11. Pythagoras.
12. Francesco Maria Della Rovere.
13. Heraclitus (Michelangelo).
14. Diogenes.
15. Euclid (Bramante).
16. Zoroaster (Pietro Bembo?).
17. Ptolemy.
18. Raphael's self-portrait.
19. Portrait of Sodoma.

Raphael
**The Stanza of the Signatura.
View of the Stanza
with the "School of Athens"
and "Parnassus"**

⇨
Raphael
**The Stanza
of the Signatura.
The School
of Athens** (detail)

Socrates conversing with Xenophon, Aeschines, and Alcibiades. In the foreground to the left, Averroes, and Francesco Maria Della Rovere.

mystery of the Eucharist. Thanks to Vasari who provided a lengthy (although not always accurate) description of the Stanzas, we can identify the personalities in this group. "There are", writes Vasari, "Dominic, Francis, Thomas Aquinas, Bonaventure, Scotus, Niccolò de Lira, Dante (considered a theologian by his contemporaries), Fra' Girolamo Savonarola da Ferrara, and all the Christian theologians plus an infinity of portraits". The last observation is interesting; in fact, on the far left, the aged Dominican with eyes raised to heaven is probably Fra' Angelico; St. Gregory, intently contemplating the Host, has the features of Julius II; on the right, we easily recognize the dignified, solemn figure of Sixtus IV, the uncle of Julius II; behind Sixtus is the laurel-crowned Dante; and finally, Savonarola almost entirely covered by his black hood.

The carefully planned and balanced composition suggests the strong influence of Perugino; but it already enjoys that harmony which Raphael went on to perfect in his next work, the *School of Athens*.

This fresco represents natural Truth. Under the vault of an immense basilica (inspired by Constantine's in the Roman Forum), decorated with statues of Apollo and Minerva, a crowd of philosophers and wise men of the past argue heatedly among themselves or meditate in silence. In the center we see Plato (long white beard and the features of Leonardo da Vinci), text of the *Timaeus* in hand, the other hand pointing to heaven, the "seat of the ideas". At his side is

(continuation, see p. 151)

Raffaello
The Stanza of the Signatura.
"The School of Athens"

146

Raphael
The Stanza of the Signatura.
The School of Athens (detail)

Raphael and Sodoma.

⇐

Raphael
The Stanza of the Signatura.
The School of Athens (detail)

Heraclitus portrayed with the features of Michelangelo Buonarroti.

Aristotle in turn holding his *Ethics* and pointing to the earth. The two philosophers and their graphic gesturing make a point which is the core of the philosophy of Marsilio Ficino: Aristotle's gesture symbolizes the positive spirit; the vertical gesture of Plato alludes to a superior quality, the contemplation of ideas.

After Vasari, others have tried to identify the personalities in the central group, but there continues to be disagreement among scholars. On the left, cloaked in olive mantle, is Socrates (faun-like profile) arguing in a group that includes Chrysippus, Xenophon, Aeschines and Alcibiades. Facing a venerable old man (Zeno?) is Epicurus, crowned with vine leaves, presumably defending hedonism. Attentively followed by his pupils (among whom is the turbanned Averroes) Pythagoras teaches the diatesseron from a book. In strong contrast in front of him is Xenocrates (others say Parmenides). In the foreground, head resting on his arm, the mournfully meditating Heraclitus. The absence of this figure in the original cartoon (now in Milan's Ambrosian Library) and the obvious Michelangelo style, lead one to believe that Raphael added this figure in 1511 when, after completing the room, he saw the first half of the Sistine Chapel ceiling. In tribute to his great rival, Raphael portrayed Michelangelo in the figure of the philosopher from Ephesus. The child at the side of Epicurus, clearly indifferent to the speculations of the philosophers, seems to be Federico Gonzaga. The passerby, in white translucent

(continuation, see p. 156)

⇨

Raphael
The Stanza of the Signatura.
The School of Athens (detail)

Euclid portrayed with the features of Bramante.
Raphael's signature stands out clearly on the collar of Euclid's tunic.

Raphael
The Stanza of the Signatura.
The wall depicting Justice (detail)

The fresco of St. Raymond of Peñafort
presenting the Decretals to Gregory IX.
Gregory IX here has the features of Pope Julius II.

155

toga and da Vinci smile, is supposedly Francesco Maria Della Rovere. Further to the right, calmly stretched out on the stairs, is Diogenes, the object of the remonstrations by the disciples of the Academy. In the foreground, to the right of Aristotle, Raphael portrayed Bramante in the person of Euclid, bending over a table and demonstrating a theorem with the help of a compass. Bramante—the great architect of Julius II—was responsible for Raphael's call to Rome. Raphael chose the gold border of Euclid's (Bramante) tunic for his own signature: R.U.S.M., that is, "Raphaël Urbinas Sua Manu" (by the hand of Raphael of Urbino). Further to the right, identified by the crown he wears, is the geographer Ptolemy (confused with the Egyptian dynasty of the same name) holding the globe of the earth. Facing him is the astronomer Zoroaster, holding the globe of the sky. The young man at their side and facing the viewer is supposedly Raphael himself in the company of Sodoma (white mantle), the artist who preceded Raphael in the decoration of the ceiling of this room.

The optical illusion in the *Dispute* and the *School ot Athens* and the impression of vastness they suggest, are not as evident on the other two walls. There were surface problems. Raphael was obliged to take into consideration the door and the window. Nevertheless, he achieved exceptional results in this less than suitable space by extending the illusion of perspective and decentralizing the compositions.

The concept of Beauty is symbolically illustrated in the *Mount Parnassus* where we see Apollo playing his lyre (sweet tones) in the presence of the nine Muses (at Apollo's feet sit the beautiful Calliope—the Muse of epic poe-

(continuation, see p. 159)

156

MOUNT PARNASSUS

1. Apollo.
2. Calliope.
3. Terpsichore.
4. Erato.
5. Polhymnia.
6. Melpomene.
7. Urania.
8. Thalia.
9. Clio.
10. Euterpe.
11. Statius.
12. Virgil.
13. Homer.
14. Dante.
15. Ennius.
16. Anacreon.
17. Petrarch.
18. Corinna.
19. Alcaeus.
20. Sappho.
21. Ariosto.
22. Boccaccio.
23. Tibullus.
24. Tebaldeo.
25. Propertius.
26. Ovid.
27. Sannazaro.
28. Horace.

←
Raphael
The Stanza of the Signatura.
View of the Stanza with "Parnassus"

Raphael
The Stanza of the Signatura.
The Parnassus (detail)
Poets in conversation and Sappho.

157

try—with horn; and Terpsichore, the Muse of lyric poetry, who holds the zither) and of great poets ancient and contemporary. We see the blind Homer scanning the sky while Ennius writes down the verses he dictates. Behind them is Dante (in cameo profile) who answers Virgil. The figure at their side is probably Statius. In the foreground and to the left is the gracefully reclining figure of Sappho, in blue and white garment with gold adornments. She turns towards Alcaeus, Corinna, Petrarch (whose head can be seen peeking from behind a tree) and Anacreon. Identifying the figures on the opposite side is more difficult; the fifth from the end (white beard, profile) could be Tebaldeo facing Boccaccio, Tibullus, and Ariosto. In the foreground, finger to his lips, is Ovid; together with Sannazaro, he converses with Horace.

On the opposite lunette, the *Cardinal and Theological Virtues* represent *subjective* Good. Strength holds an oak branch (crest of Julius II Della Rovere); Prudence, shown with two faces, looks intently into a mirror; while Temperance holds the reins. Justice is portrayed on the ceiling of this room. Faith, Hope, and Charity—the theological virtues—are depicted as cherubs. Faith points heavenward; Hope holds a torch; and Charity shakes the acorns from the tree of Strength.

Below the window, *objective* Good, object of ecclesiastical and civil law, is illustrated by two historical scenes. To the left, *St. Ray-*

(continuation, see p. 166)

Raphael
The Stanza of the Signatura.
Mount Parnassus

The monochrome scenes on the base depict the Recovery of the Sibylline Books in the tomb of Numa; Augustus Caesar preventing the destruction of the Aeneid.

159

Raphael
The Stanza of the Signatura.
The Parnassus (detail)

A group of Muses.

Raphael
The Stanza of the Signatura.
The Parnassus

A group of poets in conversation, and Horace.

161

mond of Peñafort Presents the De-cretals to Gregory IX (another portrait of Julius II with three of his favorite cardinals—Giovanni de' Medici, later Pope Clement VII; behind him is Alexander Farnese, later Pope Paul III; and Antonio del Monte). On the right, *Emperor Justinian Hands the Pandects to Trebonianus.* These two frescoes are far below Raphael's usual standards; they were probably the work of the French artist, Guillaume de Marcillat.

The wall frescoes are Raphael's, but the ceiling was done by others. The decorative composition of the ceiling's central octagon—crests of the Church surrounded by winged

(continuation, see p. 169)

Raphael
**The Stanza of the Signatura.
The Ceiling**

The four rectangular scenes
with Adam and Eve,
the Judgment of Solomon, Astronomy,
and Apollo and Marsyas.
In the center the coat-of-arms
of Nicholas V.

162

Raphael
The Stanza of the Signatura.
The Ceiling

The four medallions from the left
depict Philosophy, Theology, Justice and Poetry.

Raphael
**The Stanza of Heliodorus.
The freeing of St. Peter**
(Acts, 12 3 sq).

164

Raphael
The Stanza of Heliodorus.
The freeing of St. Peter (detail)

The angel awakens St. Peter.

HELIODORUS PURSUED AND FELLED IN THE TEMPLE

⇨

Raphael
**The Stanza of Heliodorus.
Heliodorus pursued and felled
in the Temple** (detail)
The divine messenger on charger
pursues Heliodorus.

1. The divine messenger.
2. Heliodorus.
3. The High Priest Onias.
4. Pope Julius II.
5. Giulio Romano (Raphael?).
6. Marcantonio Raimondi.
7. G. Pietro dei Foliarii.

Raphael
**The Stanza
of Heliodorus.
View of the "Stanza
of Heliodorus" with
the Mass of Bolsena
and the expulsion of
Heliodorus**

167

N · D · M · D · X · IIII

cherubs—was there when Raphael began frescoing in 1508. He then planned the four basic ideas which his assistants reflected in the four subjects depicted on the walls. Above the *Dispute* is Theology; above the *Virtues,* Justice; above the *School of Athens,* Philosophy (flanked by the statues of Diana of Ephesus, the symbol of fertility); above the *Parnassus,* Poetry. The four rectangular scenes are also related to the same theme. Part of this work may be Sodoma's, namely *Adam and Eve* (prelude to the coming of Christ), the *Judgment of Solomon* (another aspect of objective Good), *Astronomy* (an allusion to science), and *Apollo and Marsyas* (glorifying beauty).

II. The Stanza of Heliodorus (1511-1514)

Whereas the frescoes of the first Stanza express the noblest aspects of Renaissance classical thought and its efforts to unite with the spirituality of Christian thought, the pictorial plan for the *Stanza of Heliodorus* (decorated next in point of time) illustrates God's protection over His Church since the late Middle Ages. The forceful interventions of the warrior Pope, Julius II, were a decisive factor during this time. Little wonder then that we should see here scenes of the many important events during his reign. With the change in perception, there is also a change—and increased maturity—in Raphael's style. Undisputed master of Tuscan design, the artist now concentrated on color. His genius for constant growth enables him to assimilate the skill of the Venetian masters such as Dosso, Lotto, and

Raphael
The Stanza of Heliodorus.
Heliodorus pursued and felled
in the Temple (2 Maccabees, chap. 3)

even his rival, Sebastiano del Piombo. Here too the decoration of the ceiling was left to his disciples while Raphael began with the main scene *Heliodorus Pursued and Felled in the Temple*. We see Heliodorus after he breaks into the Temple with a confederate to steal its treasures. He is pursued by the faithful and by a horseman who joins them, and falls heavily to the ground. Meanwhile, oblivious to the excitement around him, the priest Onias is deep in silent prayer near the altar. The allusion to enemies of the Church who infiltrated even the highest ranks is obvious and deliberate. But more! We find Julius II himself (carried on the pontifical chair) witnessing (and perhaps directing?) the apprehension of the bandit. At the Pope's side is the prelate G. Pietro dei Foliarii (the sketch is ambiguous; some believe this a Raphael self-portrait); the two chair-bearers are traditionally identified as the engraver Marcantonio Raimondi, and Giulio Romano (here again some claim to recognize the features of Raphael). The whole fresco celebrates the finely honed skill of consummate composition: the violent diagonal movement rushing towards Heliodorus and then subtly repeated in the group clinging to the column; the open space in the center, revealing a deep perspective; on the opposite side, the rhythmic solemnity of the papal group and then the frightened women crouching alongside. Light accentuates the most dramatic segments of the action while the priest Onias has only the shadowy glimmer from the candelabra on the altar.

The *Mass at Bolsena* illustrates the miracle experienced by a priest from Bohemia who doubted the real presence of Christ in the Eucharist and then saw real blood issuing from the Sacred Host during

his celebration of Mass at Bolsena. The miraculous event prompted Urban IV to institute the Feast of Corpus Christi which Sixtus IV revived. The fresco then is a tribute to the first Della Rovere Pope (Sixtus IV) and, at the same time, a commemoration of the successful Council of 1512. Again Raphael portrays Julius II (this time we find him to the right of the altar). Behind him are the aged Cardinal Riario and Cardinal Sangiorgio. As with *Parnassus,* Raphael found a difficult surface area to work on: it was broken with a window which itself was not even centered. He camouflaged this drawback by designing the stairs asymmetrically. The result shows great strength in composition and enhances the dynamism of its parts. With his range of colors, Raphael achieves extraordinary pure effects; one is led to think of some Venetian artist—a Lotto, for example—who at the time was in Rome. It is claimed that Lotto was responsible for the dark hues of the velvet worn by the Swiss Guards on the right side.

The subject of the next fresco is the *Meeting of Leo I and Attila.* (The event took place near Mantua, not at the gates of Rome as Raphael's painting would lead us to believe). The historical encounter marked the end of the Hunnish invasion when St. Peter and St. Paul appeared to Attila. The calm, dignified figure of the Pope and his court contrasts sharply with the excited agitation of the barbarians. Again, the Pope has the features of Julius II (an obvious allusion to the Battle of Ravenna in 1512). Behind the Pope stands Car-

(continuation, see p. 174)

Raphael
**The Stanza of Heliodorus.
Heliodorus pursued and felled
in the Temple** (detail)

Portrait of Julius II and the chair-bearers Marcantonio Raimondi and Giulio Romano.

Raphael
The Stanza of Heliodorus.
The Mass of Bolsena

Julius II with senior prelates of the Pontifical Court
and officers of the Swiss Guard.

⇨
Raphael
The Stanza of Heliodorus.
The Mass at Bolsena (detail)
The Swiss Guards.

173

dinal Medici, later to become Pope Leo X; further away is Paris de' Grassi. After the death of Julius II in March, 1513, his features were painted over in this scene and the likeness of the new Pope replaced it. Giovanni de' Medici therefore appears twice!

Raphael continued to give freer reign to his pupils, leaving to them the greater part of the execution. The lyric quality of the landscape in the distant horizon suggests the hand of Lorenzo Lotto.

In the last fresco of the *Stanza of Heliodorus,* Raphael again revolutionized his style and created the incomparable masterpiece, the *Liberation of St. Peter.* The setting was suggested by the titular church of Julius II, the Church of St. Peter in Chains. The painting is unlike anything in the history of art. Drawing inspiration from the *Acts of the Apostles,* the artist narrates how an angel frees St. Peter from his chains and leads him into the city while the guards are soundly asleep. Unusually striking is the contrasting intensity of the lights—from the illumination of the torch, from the moon, from the rays of breaking day, and from the almost phosforescent white of the angel. This mastery cannot be explained by a simple referral to the nightlight effects created by Piero della Francesca in the "Dream of Constantine" (preserved in Arezzo), as many scholars have done.

The paintings on the ceiling were done before Raphael. There is sufficient affinity of style between them and the two scenes relating to Justice in the *Stanza of the Signatura* to attribute both to the hand of Guillaume de Marcillat.

(continuation, see p. 176)

Raphael
The Stanza of Heliodorus.
St. Leo the Great's Meeting with Attila
(detail)

Attila and his suite.

ST. LEO THE GREAT CONFRONTS ATTILA

1. Pope Leo X.
2. Cardinal Giovanni de' Medici (future Leo X).
3. The Master of Ceremonies, Paris de' Grassi.
4. The Chamberlain, G. Lazzaro de' Magistris (called Serapica).
5. St. Peter.
6. St. Paul.
7. The Colosseum.
8. Attila the Hun.

Raphael
The Stanza of Heliodorus.
St. Leo the Great's Meeting with Attila (detail)

Portrait of Pope Leo X, Cardinal Giovanni de' Medici and suite.

Just as in the *Stanza of the Signatura,* the four episodes re-echo the large-scale scenes on the walls: the Burning Bush testifies to the power of God, invisible here as He was when Heliodorus was expelled from the Temple. *Jacob's Ladder* appears in a vision as did the angel to St. Peter. *God Appears to Noah,* allowing him to save the world, just as heavenly intervention put an end to the invasion of the Huns under Attila. Finally, the *Sacrifice of Abraham* is a witness to blind faith, to which the priest of the Bolsena Mass also gave proof.

III. The Stanza of the Borgo Fire
(1514-1517)

The third Stanza worked on (the first in topographical order) further develops the political theme begun in the *Stanza of Heliodorus.* The events, however, have Leo X as the protagonist; he himself suggested the plan. The frescoes take events from the lives of two Popes of the same name—Leo III and Leo IV bearing the features of Leo X. The painting alludes to contemporary events. Raphael no longer has full direction of his pupils; they slowly free themselves from his influence and develop their own personal styles under the direction of Giulio Romano and Gianfrancesco Penni. Little wonder. Raphael was given other responsibilities in Rome at the time: in 1514 he took over from Bramante as chief architect of the new St. Peter's then being built; moreover, the following year he was named superintendent of antiquities. From this time he was perforce more concerned about architecture and antiquities than

(continuation, see p. 180)

Raphael
The Stanza of Heliodorus.
St. Leo the Great's Meeting with Attila

LEO·PP·X·ANN·

View of the Ceiling of the Stanza of Heliodorus

The four scenes depict the Burning Bush, the Sacrifice of Abraham, Noah leaving the Ark, and the Dream of Jacob.

Raphael
The Stanza of the Borgo Fire. The Coronation of Charlemagne
(The inscription below reads:
Charlemagne, the sword and the shield of the Roman Church).

about the frescoes which he could only occasionally supervise and to which he could rarely add his personal touch.

According to a pasage in the *Liber Pontificalis,* the *Borgo Fire* occurred near the Vatican in 847 and was extinguished by the solemn blessing of Leo IV imparted from the Vatican Palace. The edifice depicted is the old Constantinian Basilica with the mosaic façade; it was razed early in the 16th century to make room for the new St. Peter's on which Raphael (after Bramante) was working. Roman monuments are clearly in evidence, but the setting is Troy. One of the most beautiful groupings illustrates a passage from Virgil: the hero Aeneas flees the city carrying his father Anchises on his shoulders while his little son, Ascanius, scurries alongside them. Together with the women in the foreground, this is without doubt, one of the Urbino Master's most impressive efforts. But the figures jumping from the wall betray a departure from classical harmony and a decline into "Mannerism". Giulio Romano contributed the imposing and dramatic figure of the woman carrying water. The *Liber Pontificalis* also supplied information about the *Battle of Ostia* when, in 849, Leo IV and his army opposed the Saracen hordes. The fray composed with consummate skill, is dominated by the imperious figure of Leo X. It is highly probable that Giulio Romano not only executed the painting, but was also the original designer of the work.

The other two scenes are notably weak. The first is the *Coronation of Charlemagne by Leo III*

(continuation, see p. 185)

Raphael
The Stanza of the Borgo Fire.
The Borgo Fire.

180

Raphael

The Stanza of the Borgo Fire. The Borgo Fire (detail)

Carrying his father Anchises on his shoulders, Aeneas flees the city with his son Ascanius.

Raphael
The Stanza of the Borgo Fire. The Borgo Fire (detail)
Pope Leo IV imparting his blessing. On the left, the facade of the old St. Peter's Basilica.

Raphael
The Stanza of the Borgo Fire.
The Battle of Ostia

On the left, Leo X is portrayed in the person of Leo IV.

⇨
Raphael
The Stanza of the Borgo Fire.
The Oath of Leo III (detail)

The Pope is portrayed with the features of Leo X. Depicted on the ornamental front of the altar is the martyrdom of St. Catherine of Alexandria.

(probably a reference to the 1515 concordat signed by Leo X and Francis I) —a collaboration between the artists Penni and Raffaellino del Colle. The second represents the *Oath of Leo III,* who responded to the slanderous accusations of the nephews of Adrian I, reaffirming the principle that the Vicar of Christ is responsible to God alone. It is generally agreed that Alfonso di Ferrara is portrayed in the person of the emperor and Lorenzo de' Medici in that of the accuser.

Apparently because he lost interest (or did not have the time to retain interest) in decorative painting, Raphael left untouched the Holy Trinity frescoes on the ceiling. They were executed by Perugino, Raphael's master and predecessor, between 1507 and 1508.

IV. The Stanza of Constantine (1517-1524)

Projected to illustrate the defeat of paganism and the triumph of Christianity, the frescoes in this room continue and complete the political theme of the two preceding rooms. Commissioned by Leo X in 1517, Raphael barely had time to plan the design and decoration before his untimely death, April 6, 1520. The paintings, completed in 1524, were entirely the work of his pupils.

The *Battle at the Milvian Bridge* (today's Ponte Molle) dominates everything in this Stanza: in 312, Constantine opposes and defeats Maxentius. The great crowd of participants in this scene filled with movement is etched as if in classic relief, modelled after Trajan's column; still, everything centers on the majestic, self-assured figure of Constantine. The original design, as we mentioned earlier, was Raphael's; but the somewhat rhetori-

(continuation, see p. 191)

**The Stanza of the Borgo Fire.
View of the Ceiling**

The four medallions, the work of his predecessor Pietro Perugino, were
retained by Raphael. They show God the Creator and angels, Christ
between the Baptist and Satan disguised as an old man, the Holy Trinity
and the Apostles; and Christ in glory.

Within the fresco:

LAVACRVM
RENASCEN
TIS VITAE
C·VAL
CONSTANTINI

CLEMENS·VII
PONT MAX
A LEONE X
COEPTVM
CONSVMMAVIT
MDXXIIII

**The Stanza of Constantine.
The Baptism of Constantine**

The Stanza of Constantine.
The Cross appears to Constantine

Inscribed across the ray of light are the words: "In this sign you shall conquer".

The Stanza of Constantine.
Full view of the Ceiling

In the center, The "Triumph of Christianity over Paganism" painted by Tommaso Siciliano, disciple of Sebastiano del Piombo. The painter was commissioned by Gregory XIII and Sixtus V. The figures on the sides allude to the glory of these two Popes.

MVLIAE·A·CONSTANTINO
MAGNO·ECCLESIAE·IN
EVROPA·AEDIFICATAE
A·QVO·EJCINIVS
IN·CRVCIS·SIGNO·VICTVS
SVAE·IN·CHRISTIANOS
IMMANITATIS·POENAS
DEDIT

AVG·ET·TIB·IMPP·CRVCI·SVBICIVNTVR

ANNO DÑI
MDLXXXV

C·VAL·AVREL·CONSTANTINI
IMP·VICTORIA·QVA·SVBMERSO
MAXENTIO·CRISTIANORVM
OPES·FIRMATAE·SVNT

On the fresco: **PONT·SVI PRIMO**

cal style in execution reveals the firmly established personality of Giulio Romano. We detect a strong trace of Mannerism, the dominant feature in painting for the next three generations, until the Counter-Reformation.

The *Vision of the Cross,* that the Emperor received as he briefed his troops before the battle, was his personal assurance of victory. The scene faithfully mirrors the details related in the ancient "cohortationes". The studied, lavish tone — epitomizing Mannerism — once again reveals the hand of Giulio Romano. In plain contrast is the deformed dwarf in the foreground — Cardinal de' Medici's jester.

The *Donation of Rome,* probably a collaboration between Giulio Romano and Raffaellino del Colle, recounts the legend of Constantine's gift of temporal power to Pope Silvester I. The power is symbolized by the small statue of the goddess Roma. Vasari claimed to have recognized contemporary artists in this fresco; today's scholars doubt the substance of these claims. At most, they recognize Giulio Romano (raising his hand to his cap) in the figure at the second column on the right.

In the fourth fresco we see the *Baptism of Constantine* in the Lateran baptistery. Pope Silvester bears the features of Clement VII. The style of this composition is unlike any other: a hesitant and weak thrust both in design and color recalls the style of Gianfrancesco Penni. The most faithful of Raphael's disciples, he was also the most retiring of the group. To sum up, the frescoes of this Stanza are only a reminder of Raphael's style.

Raphael
The Stanza of Constantine.
The Battle at the Milvian Bridge

Raphael
**Vatican Picture Gallery.
The Crowning of the Virgin**

Painted by Raphael before he was twenty years old. The inspiration, composition and coloring of the work show the clear influence of the School of Perugino, but there is already evidence of the unmistakeable style that Raphael would bring to painting. The work dates from 1502 and was executed for Maddalena degli Oddi.

Raphael
**Vatican Picture Gallery.
The Adoration of the Magi**

Flanked by the Annunciation and the Presentation in the Temple, it formed the center panel of the altarpiece of the Crowning of the Virgin (adjoining page). It measures 27 by 150 cm, and has been separated from the Crowning. Even more than the Crowning of the Virgin, it shows that detachment which would carry Raphael further and further away from the tired style of Umbrian painting.

Raphael
**Vatican Picture Gallery.
The Madonna of Foligno**

Painted in 1511-1512 for Sigismondo de' Conti, who had escaped unharmed when his house in Foligno was struck by lightning (the event is seen in the background). The donor is shown kneeling and being presented to the Blessed Virgin by Saint Jerome (below, right). On the left are Saints John the Baptist and Francis. The painting has a sweetness and harmony of color typical of Raphael.

Raphael
**Vatican Picture Gallery.
The Transfiguration**

This painting was left unfinished by Raphael at his death in 1520, and was completed by Giulio Romano and G F. Penni. The upper part portrays the scene on Mount Tabor: Jesus, between Moses and Elijah, is transfigured before His disciples. In the lower part the apostles are struggling with a lunatic. Contrasts of light and movement between the two scenes create a spectacular and dramatic whole. Thanks to skilful restoration by the Vatican Museums, the painting has regained its pristine splendor.

THE RAPHAEL LOGGIAS

The Raphael Loggias are unquestionably one of the most representative monuments in the classic Italian Renaissance tradition. When Julius II commissioned Bramante to build a series of superimposed loggias in 1512, he had in mind a façade for the eastern side of the former palace of Pope Nicholas III. Bramante continued the work under the reign of Leo X and, when he died, the responsibility for the entire enterprise passed on to Raphael. Vasari writes that Raphael worked "with greater sense of order and decoration", apparently because he drew more deeply from ancient Roman architecture. Raphael completed the second floor loggia—which is linked with his name—and built still another above it.

Raphael at this time was the official papal architect and also the superintendent general of antiquities. No wonder then that the loggias should reveal so profound an understanding of ancient Roman art. The whole façade structure with its super-imposed loggias clearly evokes the design of such monuments as the Theater of Marcellus and the Colosseum. There too we see the prominent succession of the three orders of columns: the Doric, the Ionic, and the Corinthian. The triple series of arches forms one single series of three open loggias, superimposed over each other—an ideal passage-way between the Vatican Palace and the panorama of Rome spreading out through the arches.

The Raphael Loggias consist of thirteen arches forming a gallery 65 meters long and 4 meters wide. The pictorial decoration probably was initiated in 1517. The 1513 date, inscribed on the left side of the window in the twelfth arch, probably refers to the beginning of the pontificate of Leo X. In each of the first twelve small arches, Raphael used illustrations inspired by the Old Testament; in the thirteenth, he chose four scenes taken from the New Testament. He probably chose these specific religious subjects in a spirit of competition, challenge—a contest between himself and Michelangelo, between paintings in the Loggias and those completed several years previously in the Sistine Chapel. The 52 scenes on the ceilings of the Loggias are still popularly referred to as "the Raphael Bible".

The construction of the new St. Peter's Basilica and the paintings in the Stanzas were burden enough, so that Raphael was almost physically unable to take part in the execution of the frescoes in the Loggias. He simply had to be content preparing the design and supervising the actual work. Vasari informs us that there were numerous collaborators. Besides the faithful Gian-

(continuation, see p. 199)

External view of the Loggias

Raphael, who had replaced Bramante as supervisor of the project, finished the second Loggia and following the principles of Vitruvius topped the entire construction in 1519 with a trabeated peristyle.

The Raphael Loggias.
The decoration of the Loggias

The **Second Loggia,** on the same floor as the Apartments of Julius II and Leo X was the first to be decorated, probably beginning in 1517, by Raphael and his assistants (painters, stuccoers and masons). With this lively figurative ornamentation, clearly inspired by classical models, Raphael set the trend for so-called 'grotesque' decorations which soon became popular as wall frescoes in numerous palaces. The decoration is similar to the frescoes that had recently been uncovered in Nero's Domus Aurea; since the Domus Aurea was below ground level it was called a "grotto", hence the name of the style. Leo X had his collection of works of art arranged in the Loggia, called Raphael's Loggia. The decoration of the **First Loggia** (above, right) on the same floor as the Borgia Apartments, consists of trompe l'oeil grape arbors and grotesque patterns and is the work of Giovanni da Udine, one of Raphael's assistants, who finished it in 1519. Many years later, between 1560 and 1564, Giovanni da Udine and his assistants also decorated the **Third Loggia,** called the Cosmography Loggia, because of frescoes of maps on the walls (European, Asian and African countries), quite a novelty for the times; the maps were painted by Antonio Vanosino da Varese on cartoons by Etienne Dupérac.
Today the entrance to the Secretariat of State.

⇨
Raphael's Loggia.
View of the vault of the seventh bay

Inspired by Hellenistic themes and by the ancient stuccoes of the Colosseum, Raphael entrusted the decorative part of the Loggias to Giovanni da Udine. In the center, the coat-of-arms of Leo X. The frescoes executed by the school of Raphael illustrate scenes from the Old Testament: the temptation of Potiphar's wife, Joseph sold by his brothers, Joseph's dreams, the pharaoh's dreams.

francesco Penni, called "the Craftsman" (il Fattore) and Giulio Romano, the Master called upon Giovanni da Udine—leaving the Venetian workshop of his master, Giorgione and, in turn, da Udine brought along the Florentine, Perin del Vaga. Polidoro da Caravaggio learned his craft here, starting out as a modest color mixer for the established artists. He was later to establish himself as a foremost decorator of façades in the graffiti style. Other artists of a secondary order swelled the ranks.

Because of the close collaboration of the whole "Raphael School", it is practically impossible to distinguish the work of one or another particular artist. Though the first impression may suggest talent inferior to Raphael's, his influence and supervision seemed sufficient to reveal a strong cohesion in the pattern, even at the cost of checking the personal development of Penni, Giulio Romano, and Perin del Vaga. All of these, it is certain, were responsible for one or another part of the preparatory drawings.

The independence of Raphael's collaborators is more marked on the walls, decorated in grotesque. They drew their inspiration for this novelty from Roman paintings studied in the ruins of Nero's "Domus Aurea". The underground ruins were called grottos; hence the name "grotesque". The Raphael Loggias, however are not the first example of this imitation of the grotesques. The previous generation of artists had already been attracted by its possibilities. Pinturicchio, Perugino, Filippino Lippi, and Signorelli had already admired and worked in those chandeliers and foliages enlivened by cherubs, birds, bizarre animals, and all kinds of small objects. They enjoyed free rein for their taste for the playful and fantastic. Of the group, Giovanni da Udine displayed the keenest interest in ancient paintings. Between 1516 and 1519, he reproduced faithful imitations of this style in the decorations of the Stufetta (the bathroom) of Cardinal Bibbiena, and in the small loggia which opens on to the Perrocchetto court (buildings on the third level of the Vatican Palace, now used by the Secretariat of State of the Vatican).

Vasari tells us that Raphael was enormously pleased with his pupil and gave him the responsibility for the decoration of the rest of the Loggias. Adhering to the Master's overall plan, Giovanni da Udine designed the painting for the pillars and saw to their execution with the help of collaborators. Unfortunately, this part of the work suffered considerably from exposure to inclement weather. The problem was solved and further deterioration was checked when Pius IX closed the arches in with glass. Still, in many places the paintings are obliterated and the gilding has lost its sheen. In 1952 a fortuitous discovery was made when two half-pillars at the extreme south end of the gallery were exposed after having been walled up since the time of Paul III. We can now admire the sparkling colors of the original work. The paintings have the impression of extraordinary freshness; even the nail holes of the cartoon that guided the artist's hand are visible. These details give an idea of how great the overall beauty must have been.

Unlike the grotesque paintings of the late 15th century, those in the Loggias have a distinctive feature—medallions in stucco atop each pillar. Vasari tells us that Giovanni da Udine was fascinated by the whiteness of the ancient stuccoes, particularly those that he found in the Colosseum. After many experiments, he succeeded in rediscovering the formula. The stucco relief work adds immeasurably to the rhythmic pattern of the decoration. Standing out against the colored background of the medallions, the tiny bone white tombs, cameos, coins, suggest details of nature or scenes from every day life. We easily conjure up the vision of the artists at work: one prepares the colors, another applies the stucco to the walls. Again on the keystones of the vaults we spy small figures against the pastel backgrounds—like copies of Greek sculptures. The novelty of the composition is even more striking in the interstices of the arches. Apparently inspired by those in the Colosseum, the figures—without background color of any sort—are white on white. The neo-classical period seems to stand in the wings!

At the base of the inside walls, Perin del Vaga used bronze tones for the chiaroscuro scenes depicting episodes from the Old Testament. Hardly anything is left of this work. An excellent souvenir, however, are the few engraved copies especially Bartoli's done in the 17th century. Around this antique style of decoration —enlivened by birds, insects of all kinds, all variety of animals—Giovanni da Udine wove garlands of flowers and fruit. A feeling of cool freshness pervades the Loggias; as if one were in a greenhouse able to look up to see nature around him and the whole panorama of Rome. Reserved exclusively to the Pope, the Loggias used to be lined with ancient statues, like a private museum, where the frescoes reflected the fresh and scholarly classic Greek humanism then in vogue at the court of Leo X.

The Loggias exercised an enormous influence on art. Throughout the whole of the 16th century, artists came to copy the decorative elements in the same way as they copied the ancient Roman monuments in their quest for inspiration for the decoration of private villas. With the advent of the Baroque style in the 17th century, the fashion waned. But it was revived again at the close of the 18th century with the neo-classical period. Catherine II of Russia had an identical loggia built for herself at the Hermitage Palace, pillar for pillar, and with identical decorations on the ceilings. She commissioned the Austrian artist Unterberger to do this work. And so, the echo of the classical monument, Raphael's Loggias, reached almost to the farthest frontiers of the western world.

God separates light from darkness (1)

"When God began to create the heavens and the earth... said: 'Let there be light!'. And there was light, and God saw that the light was good. God then separated the light from the darkness" (Genesis, 1, 1, 3-4).

God separates the earth from the waters (2)

"Then God said: 'Let the waters below the sky be gathered into one place so that the dry land may appear!'... Then God said: 'Let the earth produce vegetation, seed-bearing plants and the various kinds of fruit-trees that bear fruit containing their seed!'. And so it was" (Genesis, 1, 9, 11).

Creation of the sun and moon (3)

"God made the two great luminaries, the greater luminary to rule the day and the smaller one to rule the night and the stars also. God set them in the firmament of the sky to shed light on the earth, to rule by day and by night, and to separate the light from the darkness" (Genesis, 1, 16-18).

Creation of the animals (4)

"Then God said: 'Let the waters teem with shoals of living creatures, and let birds fly over the earth across the firmament of the sky!'... God made the various kinds of wild beasts of the earth, the various kinds of domestic animals, and all the various kinds of land reptiles" (Genesis, 1, 20, 25).

Creation of Eve (5)

"Then the Lord God had a trance fall upon the man, and when he had gone to sleep, he took one of his ribs, closing up its place with flesh. The rib which he took from the man the Lord God built up into a woman" (Genesis, 2, 21, 22).

Original sin (6)

"So when the woman realized that the tree was good for food and attractive to the eye, and further, that the tree was desirable for its gift of wisdom, she took some of its fruit, and ate it, she also gave some to her husband with her, and he ate" (Genesis, 3, 6).

Adam and Eve banished from Eden (7)

"So the Lord God expelled him from the garden of Eden, to till the ground from which he had been taken, he drove the man out, and stationed the cherubim east of the garden of Eden, with the flaming, whirling sword to guard the way to the tree of life" (Genesis, 3, 23, 24).

Building the ark (9)

"So God said to Noah: 'I have resolved on the extermination of all mortals; for the earth is full of wrongdoing through them; I am going to exterminate them from the earth. Make yourself an ark of oleander wood; make the ark with cabins, and smear it with bitumen inside and out...' Noah did so; he did just as God had commanded him" (Genesis, 6, 13, 14, 22).

Abraham and Melchisedech (13)

"On his return from the defeat of Chedorlaomer and his confederate kings, the king of Sodom came out to the valley of Shaveh... to meet him, while Melchisedech, king of Salem, brought out bread and wine, and, as priest of God Most High, blessed him, saying: 'Blessed be Abram by God Most High'" (Genesis, 14, 17-19).

Abraham and three Angels (15)

"The Lord appeared to him by the terebinth of Mamre. Raising his eyes, he saw three men standing near him. On seeing them, he ran from the door of his tent to meet them, and bowing to the earth said: 'O sirs, if perchance I find favor with you, please do not pass by without stopping with your servant'" (Genesis, 18, 1-3).

Lot flees from Sodom (16)

"When dawn appeared, the angels urged Lot on... Just as the sun rose over the earth and Lot entered Zoar, the Lord rained sulphur and fire from the sky on Sodom and Gomorrah, devastating those cities and all the valley... And Lot's wife had looked back, and had become a pillar of salt" (Genesis, 19, 15, 24-26).

God appears to Isaac (17)

"The Lord then appeared to him, and said: '... I will make your descendants as numerous as the stars in the sky, and I will give your descendants this whole country, so that all the nations of the earth will invoke blessing on one another through your descendants'" (Genesis, 26, 2, 4).

Jacob meets Rachel (22)

"While he was still talking... Rachel arrived with her father's flock... As soon as Jacob saw Rachel... Jacob went up, and rolling the stone off the mouth of the well, watered the flock of Laban, his mother's brother. Then Jacob kissed Rachel, and lifted up his voice in weeping" (Genesis, 29, 9-11).

The dreams of Joseph (25)

"Joseph had a dream, which he told to his brothers, so that they hated him all the more... Then he had another dream which he recounted to his brothers: 'I have just had another dream', he said 'and the sun, moon, and eleven stars made obeisance to me!' " (Genesis 27, 5, 9).

The dreams of the Pharaoh (28)

"Joseph said to Pharaoh: 'Pharaoh's dream is simple, God would reveal to Pharaoh what he is about to do. The seven fat cows represent seven years, and the seven plump ears of corn represent seven years... The seven lean and ugly cows that came up after them represent seven years, and so do the seven empty ears of corn blasted by the east wind; there are to be seven years of famine'" (Genesis 41, 25-27).

Moses saved from the water (29)

"Presently Pharaoh's daughter came down to bathe at the Nile, while her maids walked on the bank of the Nile. Then she saw the ark among the reeds and sent her maid to get it" (Exodus, 2, 5).

The waters gushing from the rock (32)

"The Lord said to Moses: 'Pass on ahead of the people, taking with you some of the elders of Israel; take the staff in your hand with which you struck the Nile, and go on. I will station myself there before you on the rock at Horeb, and when you strike the rock, water will gush out of it, so that the people may drink'" (Exodus, 17, 5, 6).

Adoring the golden calf (34)

"Moses then turned and descended from the mountain, with the two tablets of the decrees in his hand. As soon as he came near the camp, he saw the calf and the dancing, whereupon Moses' anger blazed, and he flung the tablets from his hand, and broke them at the foot of the mountain, then he took the calf which they had made, and burned it up" (Exodus, 32, 15, 19, 20).

Moses shows his people the tablets (36)

"When Moses descended from Mount Sinai. Aaron and the Israelites all saw that the skin of Moses' face was in a glow, and they were afraid to approach him... After that all the Israelites came up, and he enjoined on them all the things about which the Lord had conversed with him on Mount Sinai" (Exodus, 34, 29, 30, 32).

Crossing the river (37)

"When the people left their tents to cross the Jordan... The priests carrying the ark of the covenant of the Lord took their stand on dry ground, right in the middle of the Jordan, while all Israel crossed over on dry ground, until the whole nation had finished crossing the Jordan" (Joshua, 3, 14, 17).

The fall of Jericho (38)

"The seventh time the priests blew the horns, and then Joshua said to the people: 'Shout; for the Lord is giving you the city'. So the people shouted, when the horns were blown. As soon as the people heard the sound of the horns, the people raised a mighty shout, and the wall fell flat" (Joshua, 6, 16, 20).

Joshua stops the sun (39)

"It was on the day that the Lord put the Amorites at the mercy of the Israelites that Joshua spoke to the Lord, and in the presence of Israel said: 'O sun, stop at Gibeon; and thou moon, at the valley of Aijalon!' So the sun came to a stop and the moon stood still, until the nation took vengeance on their foes" (Joshua, 10, 12-13).

Dividing the Promised Land (40)

"Then the whole Israelite community assembled at Shiloh, and set up the tent of meeting there, the region having been brought into subjection to them... So Joshua cast lots for them at Shiloh before the Lord; and there Joshua distributed the land among the Israelites, to each his share" (Joshua, 18, 1, 10).

Samuel anoints David king (41)

"Samuel... purified Jesse and his sons and invited them to the sacrifice... 'Are these all the young men?' Samuel said to Jesse. 'There is still the youngest', he said, 'but just now he is shepherding the flock'. So he sent and brought him in. Now he was ruddy, a youth with beautiful eyes and attractive appearance... then Samuel took the horn of oil and anointed him in the midst of his brothers" (1 Samuel, 16, 4, 5, 11-13).

David slays Goliath (42)

"Now when the Philistine arose and came and drew near to meet David... David put his hand in his bag and took from it a stone and slung it and it struck the Philistine on his forehead; and the stone sank into his forehead, so that he fell on his face to the earth" (1 Samuel, 17, 48-49).

David and Bathsheba (44)

"Then one day at sunset, David got up from his couch, and walked to and fro upon the roof of the king's house; and from the roof he saw a woman bathing. The woman was very beautiful... So David sent messengers and took her; and she came to him, and he lay with her" (2 Samuel, 11, 2, 4).

Solomon consecrated king (45)

"Accordingly Zadok the priest, and Nathan the prophet, and Benaiah, the son of Jehoiada, together with the Cherethites and the Pelethites, caused Solomon to ride on the mule of King David, and brought him to Gihon. Then Zadok the priest took a horn of oil from the tent and anointed Solomon" (1 Kings, 1, 38-39).

The queen of Sheba (47)

"Now when the queen of Sheba heard of the fame of Solomon through the name of the Lord, she came to test him with hard questions. So she came to Jerusalem with a very large retinue, with camels bearing spices and very much gold and precious stones; and when she came to Solomon, she conversed with him about all that was in her mind" (1 Kings, 10, 1-2).

The Epiphany of Christ (50)

"Now after the birth of Jesus at Bethlehem... astrologers from the east arrived at Jerusalem, and asked: 'Where is the newly born king of the Jews?' ... And they went into the house and saw Him with His mother, Mary, and they threw themselves down and did homage to Him. They opened their treasure boxes and presented the child with gifts of gold, frankincense, and myrrh" (Matthew, 2, 1, 2, 11).

⇨
Raphael's Loggia. A view of the vault of the thirteenth bay

It illustrates four episodes from the life of Christ: the Nativity, the Epiphany, the Baptism and the Last Supper.

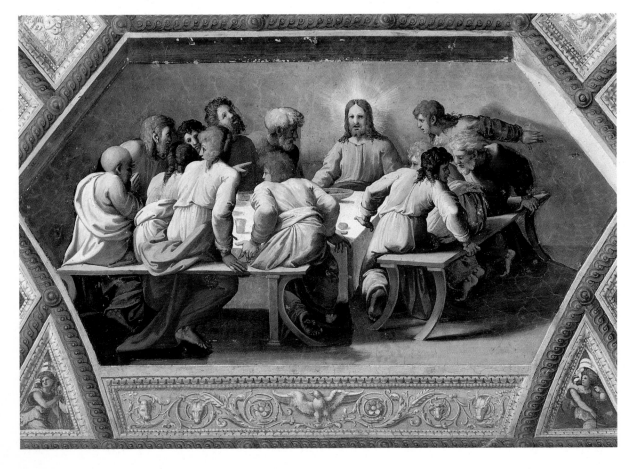

The Last Supper (52)

"When evening came, He took His place at table with the twelve disciples. As they were eating Jesus took a loaf and blessed it, and He broke it in pieces and gave it to His disciples, saying: 'Take this and eat it. It is my body!' And He took the winecup and gave thanks and gave it to them, saying: 'You must all drink from it'" (Matthew, 26, 20, 26, 27).

215

TABLE OF CONTENTS

Raphael
Vatican Picture Gallery – Charity, 1507
Oil tempera on wood – 18 × 44 cm.

TIPOGRAFIA VATICANA – 2001
CITTÀ DEL VATICANO